TEACHING CHILDREN

about

GLOBAL AWARENESS

~

TEACHING CHILDREN

about

GLOBAL AWARENESS

A Guide for Parents and Teachers

~

LAURA MEAGHER

CROSSROAD • NEW YORK

For my parents,
Marie and Fred Youngblood

1991

The Crossroad Publishing Company
370 Lexington Avenue, New York, NY 10017

Copyright © 1991 by Laura Meagher

Printed in the United States of America
Typesetting output: TEXSource, Houston

Library of Congress Cataloging-in-Publication Data

Meagher, Laura.
    Teaching children about global awareness: a guide for parents and
teachers / Laura Meagher.
      p. cm.
    Includes bibliographical references.
    ISBN 0-8245-1085-2
    1. International education—United States. I. Title.
LC1090.M387 1991
370.11′5—dc20
                                          90-22309
                                              CIP

Contents

~

Preface

~

IN THE 1950s, when I was growing up, the world was a predictable place. The United States was the center of the globe, and President Eisenhower was a beloved father figure who was occasionally criticized in the press for spending too much time on the golf course.

There was, of course, the threat of atheistic communism emanating from the enemy, Russia. We practiced diving under our desks or huddling in school corridors against the possibility of bomb attacks, and we prayed for the conversion of Russia at the end of every Mass. Everything was under control.

John F. Kennedy was inaugurated president during my senior year in high school. My classmates and I, inspired by his youth and idealism, graduated with the firm belief that we could change the world for the better. Through the Peace Corps, we could bring the blessings of the U.S. experience to developing nations.

Kennedy was assassinated while I was in college, and much of our idealism died with him. Within a decade, the racism, sexism, and militarism endemic in U.S. society were under attack. My first child was born during the Six-Day War in Israel, the forgotten impetus for much of the international terrorism that has occurred in the ensuing decades. Before my second child could walk, the man who had served as Eisenhower's vice-president resigned the presidency in disgrace, casting a pall of suspicion on the integrity of those in government service.

The United States was no longer at the center of the globe. Around the world, developing nations struggled to achieve national identities in the face of overwhelming economic and social problems. Advances in communications technology shrank boundaries at the same time that global economies became more interdependent. Problems became global in context. (In 1986, the Union of International Associations in Brussels drew up a list of ten thousand world problems — and these were only the major ones.)

Possibilities multiplied, too. Advances in health care promised more meaningful lives to millions. A new sense of the equality of all humans, regardless of gender or color, gave dignity to many who had been oppressed.

In the midst of all these changes, U.S. astronauts brought back from space a never-before-seen view of our planet: a beautiful, vulnerable orb floating in the inky darkness of space. For the first time, we saw ourselves as we are: a people linked by the destiny we shape for our common home.

As I write these words, the desire for freedom is breaking down walls of oppression all over the world faster than anyone could have imagined. It is an exciting, hopeful, but frightening time. How can we prepare our children to live in a world whose shape we cannot predict from one week to the next? Where can we look for leadership? What do we need to teach our children to give them the confidence to shape the world of the twenty-first century? What do we need to know to understand what is going on in the world and to contribute to its destiny?

My parents and teachers did not have the answers to those questions, and neither do I. But they did prepare me well to face the future with confidence in spite of all the changes that have occurred in my lifetime. When I started school, white children did not go to school with black children and Catholics did not go to other churches. Today, the governor of my state is black and the churches in my community are united in their common concerns over the issues of housing the homeless and feeding the hungry. My parents and teachers modeled the attitudes and gave me the resources to be part of the generation that has helped to bring about these changes.

We do not need to know the future in order to prepare our children to shape it. We do need to give them the global perspective they will need to shape their world. This book will suggest ways we can teach that perspective.

These suggestions are the results of my own reflections as a parent and educator. Because my perspective on the world has been profoundly shaped by my Christian faith, my views are often expressed in terms of faith. I invite you to reflect on my ideas from the perspective of your own worldview, whatever it may be. I hope you will discover that we share a common understanding of the importance of developing global awareness in our children.

To parents and teachers already overwhelmed by the daily demands of raising and educating children, the challenges of developing global awareness in our children may seem too burdensome and time-consuming. We may feel ill-prepared for the job. What this book will show is that we are better equipped for the task than we know and that it is the most important task we face in terms of preparing our children for the future. We will develop a definition of global awareness that is "close to home." We will look at the components of education for global awareness that are potentially present in family dynamics and in the classroom. We will discover ways to incorporate a global perspective into family and school life. Suggestions and resources for further exploration of basic concepts will provide opportunities for pursuing particular areas of interest. We won't solve any world problems, but we may find some ways to think about them for the future so that our children can solve them. We may even acquire an exciting new view of family life and of classroom dynamics!

We can take inspiration for the task from a favorite myth of both adults and children. *The Wizard of Oz* tells the story of a child thrust into an unfamiliar world who wants to return to her familiar home. She meets three characters who are unable to help her because they are paralyzed into inaction by their perceived lacks of intellect, emotion, and courage. Together they travel in search of one who can tell them what to do. The Wizard's response is both disconcerting and reassuring: what you need was in you all the time.

Our children *can* feel at home in a world of diverse cultures and interdependent systems. We *do* have the minds, the hearts, and the capacity to introduce them to it.

We need only to begin.

Now.

Chapter 1

Why Teach Global Awareness?

∼

ANUCLEAR ACCIDENT occurs at Chernobyl, Russia. Weeks later, livestock in Finland sicken and die.

Global emissions of carbon dioxide set a record of six billion tons in 1988. Forests in the United States and Europe die, and Mexico City suffocates slowly under a blanket of filthy, stagnant air.

In 1986 and 1987, the U.S. releases government-held rice and increases price supports for rice farmers in the U.S. in an attempt to gain a larger portion of the world rice market. The demand for rice from Thailand drops, and four million Thai farmers suffer. Children in the U.S. sing the Disney-inspired tune "It's a Small World After All." Teenagers join with the Live-Aid effort to halt starvation in Africa and sing "We Are the World." But young adults in the U.S. aged eighteen to twenty-four place last in a survey of geographical knowledge among nations polled by the Gallup organization for the National Geographic Society.

We need more than songs to make our children aware that we are living in an age of interdependent global systems.

Education as Empowerment

Why global awareness education? If the purpose of education is empowerment, the need for empowerment begins with mastery of one's environment. The very first developmental task of the child is to learn to trust the world around him or her. Without this sense of trust, the child cannot safely move on to the tasks of developing a sense of responsibility, achieving self-esteem, acquiring a personal identity, learning to love and care for others and experiencing fulfillment in the direction that life takes. Another way of saying this is to affirm that the goal of education is to make us fully human.

Global Education from a Christian Perspective

In scriptural terms we might say that God has given us life so that we might live it to the full. Jesus was the embodiment of full humanity. His life and ministry pointed unceasingly to the meaning of God's will for us, which Jesus called the kingdom. The kingdom, he said, will be like a great feast, where all will be welcome at the table if they will come with willing hearts.

Jesus scandalized his peers by modeling this welcome when he ate with the despised and outcast of society. He touched the unclean and healed them of both illness and rejection. He fed the hungry, and there was always enough to go around. The Gospel writers stress this extravagance. At Cana, he produced enough wine to lay the village out for a week — more than enough for a wedding feast. When he shared a boy's lunch with a huge crowd, the leftovers could not be contained in the boy's basket.

This kingdom, Jesus said, is within and around you, but it is hidden. It will be revealed in God's time, God's *kairos*, the right time. Christians believe that we are called to be signs of that kingdom until it comes. We are called to the same extravagance and care for the world that Jesus preached and lived. We are not to ask who is our neighbor so as to limit our obligations. Instead, we are to love as Jesus did, without condition or conceit about our own social status. We are to open our eyes and hearts to see the love and care our unknown neighbors have for us.[1]

In this view of the goal of education, a view that is informed by Christian faith, we need to develop global awareness so that we may become fully human as God intends us to be, for the sake of promoting the dignity of every human being created in God's image.

Even without the motivation of Christian faith, global awareness is essential to a child's growth in trust. Parents teach their children to avoid danger and to take care of their bodily needs so that they may survive and live in harmony with their environment. For the same reason, children are taught how to relate appropriately to other people. They learn the values and skills of their own culture so that they can relate to a larger society and feel at home in their world.

Today children must learn to see the world as their home because their environment truly is global. They must look beyond their families, their communities, and their national boundaries to the larger society that is connected not only by a common humanity but also by technology, economics, politics, environmental problems, and a shared concern for the future of the planet. They must learn to develop the basic humanitarian concerns that govern any society. When that society is global, the scope of concern must be global.

Global Awareness Education as an Economic Necessity

Much of the incentive for developing global awareness in children is coming from the realization that, as a nation, the United States has not prepared its young people to compete in a global economy. One might wish that the major incentive were a new consciousness of the problems of worldwide hunger or of the dangerous and irredeemable destruction of the environment. While there is certainly a growing concern about both these issues, the primary impetus for introducing global awareness into the educational curriculum is concern over our economic future.

Global awareness education is a means of maintaining economic leadership. When exports are vital to an economy, a global perspective is a necessary requisite for doing business. The enormous trade deficit that the United States has accrued is the result both of our habit of overconsumption of goods from all over the world and of our failure to develop markets abroad for our own consumer goods. To put the case in the most crass economic terms, we need to be concerned about the standard of living of people in other countries because poor people cannot buy what we produce. When those same poor people work for substandard wages, they are producing goods for less than what it costs to make the same items in the United States. The result is loss of jobs in the United States — and continued exploitation of Third World workers.

To compound the problem, most of the jobs lost in the United States are those that would be held by less educated people. They cannot compete against low-wage workers overseas. The globalization of the economy in this sector means a decline of wages, unemployment, and loss of productivity, with all the social problems that accompany these realities, including polarization between skilled and unskilled workers.[2] One way to make Third World wages more competitive is to be concerned about raising the living standards of workers in other countries.

"Made in the USA" is a theme that has been widely advertised as a means of promoting pride in the purchase of U.S.-manufactured products. This campaign may be an effective marketing tool, but it is a short-sighted chauvinism that attempts to preserve U.S. manufacturing jobs by shutting out goods from foreign markets. A global perspective would frame the solution in terms of increasing the incomes of people in other countries so that more U.S.-made products could be exported for sale.

Promoting the well-being of citizens of Third World countries can make good business sense. According to recent reports from the World Health Organization, about 1.3 billion people, or more than 20 percent of the world's population, are seriously sick or malnourished. Most of these people live in southern and eastern Asia and in sub-Saharan Africa, and most of their illnesses could be prevented by vaccines or treated by drugs available in First World countries.[3] Their precarious health certainly affects their productivity and their ability to provide for themselves. The present trade deficit, which amounts to billions of dollars yearly, is a reflection not only of the inability of the U.S. work force to compete in a global economy but also of the poverty of a large percentage of the world's citizens. People struggling to survive cannot purchase U.S. goods.

Exporting People

Today the world is awash in refugees, more than fifteen million of them. In addition to those who flee their homelands to escape political oppression, economic refugees seek asylum in industrialized countries in order to earn money to send back to their families in their native countries. In the United States, these hard-working individuals are often willing to take the menial jobs that no one else wants, working long hours for the sake of supporting families from whom they are separated. In several Third World countries like Pakistan or the Philippines, the government encourages citizens' dreams of working abroad because there are no jobs at home. In the meantime, the U.S. government spends time, legislative energy, and money attempting to control this influx of economic refugees, both documented and undocumented. A more productive perspective might be the global one that works to create favorable economic conditions in the native countries of these desperately poor people. In theological terms, this is called a "preferential option for the poor."

Changing Needs in a Changing World

Much of the pressure on educational institutions to increase global awareness in the curriculum is coming from the business community, and colleges and graduate schools are responding. Dr. David Blake, dean at the Edwin L. Cox School of Business at Southern Methodist University, is weaving ethical and international considerations into all the school's courses. He believes that "exposure to history, culture and political issues is crucial to international understanding." Students are required to take at least one course in international studies. Dr. Blake is also concerned that "so many students lack language ability."[4]

This concern reflects a nationwide awareness in educational circles of the increasing difficulties of competing economically abroad. A 1989 report by the National Governors Association stressed this concern. "International studies is becoming the thing that every campus wants to get on top of," says George J. Funaro, Maryland's deputy secretary of higher education. According to Mr. Funaro, the pressure is coming from the business community, searching for "more globally literate" employees.[5]

In Virginia, several colleges have opened new facilities or new programs devoted to international studies. In addition, educators across the state are developing new methods of infusing global awareness into all areas of the curriculum. Science classes take on the study of global warming and its effects on worldwide economics and politics. Math problems focus on studies of population growth. More non-Western language classes are offered. The number of credit hours of non-Western languages, particularly Japanese, offered at Virginia colleges more than tripled in the last six years. One advantage of this method of global education is that "people begin looking at the world as they're going to be living in it," according to Andrew F. Smith, director of the American Forum for Global Education.[6]

This interest in international studies is already trickling down to the high school and elementary school level, and none too soon. A Gallup survey conducted in the spring of 1989 for the National Geographic Society found that U.S. citizens ranked last of ten countries surveyed in geographic knowledge. While adults in the U.S. did better than their Soviet counterparts, Soviet students in the eighteen to twenty-four age bracket did much better than students in the U.S. Gilbert M. Grosvenor, National Geographic Society president, could not help but remark on the "astonishing ignorance of the world" by U.S. and Soviet citizens, since these "two nations are responsible for much of what happens in the world." Not surprisingly, the West Germans and the Japanese, both of whom enjoy a healthy balance of trade, achieved the best scores along with the Swedish young adults.[7]

Recent events in Eastern Europe and the breakdown of the Soviet political system offer exciting new global economic opportunities. After a period of disruption of old systems and organization of new economies, these newly-formed economic systems will seek trade and monetary links with the United States, Western Europe, and Japan. According to many economists, the Soviet Union will follow eventually. Already the European markets have announced plans to form a common economic community by 1992. "For the first time since the turn of the century, a truly global economy is about to come into existence," according to one expert.[8]

Adapting ourselves to this new economic reality is going to require some imagination from those of us who have been inclined to view the balance of power in the world in terms of the U.S.-Soviet conflict. In reality, the balance of power between the "haves" and "have-nots" has now shifted to a North-South axis. Increasingly, the "have-nots" of the world live south of the equator. In those regions, wars still rage in the pursuit of freedom and the economic opportunities that go with it. The leadership in many of these nations is anti-Western, anticapitalist and fundamentalist. One might well ask where these Third World countries fit in terms of new global economic opportunities.

Journalist Meg Greenfield asks the global questions about the new East-West realities that we need to ask ourselves as we consider new perspectives in global awareness education:

> What do we want, anyway, from and for the communist countries? What was and is the nature of their threat to us? Does the definition of our interest begin and end with protecting ourselves against aggression? Or does it also include attempting to preserve and actually extend democratic values? Do we give a hoot what kind of domestic political lives other countries lead? If Third World disputes were not overlaid with East-West meaning, would we care how they came

out? Would we be concerned only as economic interests were affected? Outside the cold-war context, does any of the currently burgeoning ethnic mayhem around the world matter to us, warfare between peoples with exotic names who have been trying to annihilate each other for centuries and whom most of us probably never even heard of until the 6 o'clock news tonight?[9]

A Question of Values

Our motives for pursuing the goals of global awareness education will shape the content of what we teach. If we are concerned about the fundamental dignity of every human being, we will be motivated by a concern for global justice and we will teach from that perspective. We will be concerned about issues that affect the Third World. If we are moved by humanitarian concerns, we will focus our teaching on the fundamental needs and rights of all people. If economic considerations are the primary incentive for acquiring a global perspective, our teaching will concentrate on the skills, information and attitudes that our young people will need to function in the international marketplace. We will concentrate on issues that affect the First World and the emerging market economies in formerly Soviet-bloc countries. Since there is no consensus on the content of global education, each of these approaches might be considered valid and valuable by some portion of the population of those who are concerned about educating for global awareness.

Who decides what is to be taught? Ultimately, our values will determine not only what is taught but how it is taught. The method of teaching in itself is an important aspect of global awareness education, as it models methods of decision-making and information-sharing that become a part of the learning experience.

Until the space age gave us a new view of our planet, most of us were inclined to view Western culture (and U.S. values) as the norm for human progress. Events of the past two decades, including the decline of our economic status in the world market, have led us to question our assumption about the superiority of our national values. While this can be a healthy and necessary corrective of a mis-centered global view, we may too hastily substitute other less desirable assumptions about global leadership if we do not name the common values that we hold as essential to our identity as citizens of the United States. At the same time that we must question assumptions that have kept us, and continue to keep us, from working for justice in the world, we also need to name the values that the U.S. has contributed to the outbreak of freedom around the globe.

In some business circles, leaders have suggested that we emulate Japanese values in order to promote economic success: hierarchy, loyalty, conformity, duty, and obedience. How do we square these values with our advocacy of freedom, equality, and justice? How do the Japanese understand civil rights, equal opportunity for women, and the right of workers to organize? Does the Japanese educational system stifle creativity or encourage it? How does the Japanese pursuit of strategic economies instead of free markets and free trade contribute to global economic development — or does it?[10] The point of these questions is not to disparage the Japanese way of doing business, but rather to suggest that we cannot embrace the practices of other cultures for the sake of economic success if it means discarding the hard-won wisdom of our own culture and experience. Global awareness education encourages us to study and learn from the wisdom of other cultures, but also to value our own and to share the best of ourselves with others. One example: Japanese businesses in the United States are buying into the U.S. tradition of corporate philanthropy. In New York City, several Japanese businesses are active in the United Way.[11]

For much of our history, we have prided ourselves on our "rugged individualism." At its best, this trait has nourished a spirit of adventure and a love of freedom that has enriched our national character. At its worst, it has made us selfish and intolerant of those who have been unable to "make it" on their own. When we make little or no effort to understand the daily struggles of people in other countries, we have little sympathy for their difficulties and we are unwilling and afraid to call them our neighbors. The times are calling for a change in this attitude, and a wonderful opportunity lies before us.

A helicopter crew that went in search of a downed U.S. aircraft in Ethiopia found this out firsthand. A thunderstorm was moving in, and they had to land in unfamiliar territory. They were afraid that they faced an unfriendly encounter. But when they climbed out of the helicopter, they were swallowed up in a sea of hugs and invited inside thatched-roof homes for food and drink. Their hosts in the village of Indibar asked them many questions — about education, and flying, and, most of all, what people thought of Ethiopia. Before their encounter, the crew members reported, they would have said "desert" and "starving people" and "disease" to describe their impressions. But they learned that the spot where they landed was lush and beautiful, and that the people valued hospitality. The pilot, Lt. Col. John Taylor, summed up the crew's feelings: "I had quite a remarkable experience. I can't say enough good things about these people."[12]

We need global awareness education to teach our children these "good things" about our unknown neighbors.

Summary

There are many reasons why global awareness education is important for children and young people. One is that global awareness is essential to the development of trust in children who live in a global environment. Another is that humanitarian concerns require an understanding of the needs and rights of every person on our endangered planet. Christians believe that God's will for every human being is fullness of life and that we are to work to promote human dignity in every corner of the globe. The most pressing incentive in our day is our growing national realization that global awareness education is a means of establishing economic leadership and of solving some of the economic problems that face the United States today. All these motivations are leading to an emphasis on promoting global awareness in school curricula at every level.

Chapter 2

What Is Global Awareness Education?

∼

Given THE PRESENT ENTHUSIASM for global awareness education, parents and educators who want to get involved can become frustrated almost immediately by the plethora of learning materials marketed as developing global awareness. Since there is at present no consensus as to the content of global awareness education, some of these claims can be misleading.

In this chapter we shall define global awareness education and consider two basic aspects of introducing children to the world: how we name it and how we see it. In the next chapter, we shall look at the content of global awareness education.

Where to Begin?

Defining global awareness education begins with defining the goals we hope to achieve by incorporating a global awareness perspective, whatever it is, into the learning experiences of our children. These can be stated rather generically as "the development in students of the knowledge, skills and attitudes needed to live effectively in a world which possesses limited natural resources and is characterized by cultural pluralism and increasing interdependence."[1] From these goals, a definition of global awareness education as a process, rather than a fixed curriculum, might be drawn to say that it is

> the lifelong growth in understanding, through study and participation, of the world community and the interdependency of its peoples and systems — ecological, social, economic and technological. Global education requires an understanding of the values and priorities of the many cultures of the world as

20

well as the acquisition of basic concepts and principles related to the world community. Global education leads to implementation of the global perspective in striving for just and peaceful solutions to world problems.[2]

The term "global education" as used in this definition can in itself be confusing if it suggests to the parent or educator the scope, rather than the process or content, of education. For example, we might speak of someone who takes a broad view of a particular issue as having a "global perspective" when we mean that he or she can see all sides of the issue, whether or not the issue itself is one that truly affects the whole world. For the sake of specificity, I prefer the term "global awareness education" because it suggests the goal, and not just the scope, of the enterprise.

What's in a Name?

The ancients believed that a person's self was contained in one's name. There is power in naming the other, since one's name affects one's self-concept. The child labeled "the smart one" tries to live up to that expectation, sometimes in spite of personal stress. A child described during the early years of school as a "slow learner" has a hard time raising expectations of his or her achievements in later years.

In the United States, we are quick to name and label realities as a way of diagnosing, analyzing, and understanding situations — and gaining control of them to our best advantage. Thus, our economy suffers from a "trade deficit," rather than a problem of overspending. Municipalities deal with the problem of "solid waste disposal," rather than name the real problem: the national habit of consumption of convenient disposables.

Naming the World

How children — and adults — see the world depends on many factors. Among the most important is the way we name it. Global awareness education begins with an understanding of the way we label other nations.

Much of the terminology we use to categorize the regions of the world is based on economic realities in terms of contrasts between the United States and other economic entities. We speak of the "haves" (rich nations) and the "have-nots" (poor nations), or of industrialized and unindustrialized nations. Poorer nations are described in terms of the achievements of richer nations, as if economic wealth were the norm and the desired goal of national development.

More Developed/Less Developed

Many educators favor the term "developing countries" for those nations that have relatively low standards of living. This term is seen as less offensive than other terms because it implies progress toward a "developed" status. The norm, however, is still the "more developed" nation, described as having high productivity, high literacy rates, low birth rates, an agricultural system that can both feed its population and export food, good educational opportunities, and well-developed communication and transportation capabilities. All of North America and Europe, the USSR, Japan, and the countries of Australasia are presently designated "more developed" by the United Nations. The rest of the world is "less developed."[3] These countries are often referred to as LDCs (less-developed countries) by economists. Theologian René Padilla calls them "the two-thirds world," an excellent reminder that the so-called developing nations are in the majority.

If the majority of the people of the world did the naming, the U.S. might be a "non-agricultural country" (NAC) that is part of the "one-third world" which relies on the "resource-rich countries" (RRCs, some of which are countries of the "two-thirds world") for many of the raw materials it needs for its industry. It's all a matter of the perspective of the ones who do the naming.

First World/Third World

Perhaps the most common categories for the countries of the world are "First World," "Second World," "Third World," and "Fourth World." The distinctions are political as well as economic.

"First World" countries are the industrialized nations that have market economies, those that allow transactions between buyer and seller to determine what goods and services are produced. Market economies are also called "capitalist" or "free enterprise" economies. First World countries are those of North America and Western Europe as well as Australia, New Zealand, and Japan. "Second World" countries are the USSR and the so-called Soviet-bloc countries of Eastern Europe that have economies controlled by the government. (At this writing, this economic system is disintegrating rapidly. What new economic forms develop in these countries remains to be seen.) "Third World" refers to the developing nations of Africa, Asia, and Latin America. "Fourth World" refers to the poorest people of the Third World; this term is seldom used.

These "First World–Third World" designations, the ones most widely used by the print and electronic media to discuss the economic and political distinctions between nations of the world, have unfortunate connotations, familiar to every child. First place is better than third place in any contest. Being "number one" is better than being "number two," even if "number two" tries harder. These distinctions are also based on a materialism that suggests that accumulation of wealth is what makes a nation "first." As one educator notes, "that association doesn't fit a scheme of things where the poor have so much to teach the rich about endurance and human dignity."[4]

While the rankings implied by the terms "first," "second," and "third" are regrettable, the term "Third World" suggests a reality that the member nations themselves have embraced. The 141 Asian, African, and Latin American member countries of the United Nations use the term collectively to describe their economic situation vis-à-vis the First World, especially to negotiate on issues relating to trade, dwindling of natural resources, and inequitable food supplies.[5] The term describes an economic reality: Third World countries are sacrificing their own sustainable development in order to satisfy the need for raw materials of First World countries.

Because it is the term preferred by member nations themselves, I use the term "Third World" when referring to "developing" countries.

East/West, North/South

During the period of time from the end of World War II until recent years, much of the emphasis in the study of global dynamics was on the East/West political dichotomy. The United States and its allies ("the West") and the Soviet Union and its allies ("the Eastern bloc") were perceived as the two major political powers on the globe during the recent period when the Cold War dominated the balance of power. While globe-threatening hostilities have been held in check, it has not been a time of peace. More than 120 "local" wars have been fought since the end of World War II.

Within recent years, the balance of power has shifted to a North/South axis. Where wars between East and West were once fought over ideological differences, new conflicts over the distribution of dwindling resources threaten world peace. For the most part, these inequities occur in a pattern that divides countries north of the equator from those south of it, where most Third World countries are located. As East/West tensions are dissipating, North/South tensions are rising.

Seeing the World

Talking about the world in particular terms gives children one understanding of global relationships, but young children will not be able to grasp many of the concepts outlined in the previous discussion. Distinctions between "rich" and "poor" are relative to elementary-age children. Many children who live in affluent households will describe themselves as poor if the income available for their personal use is inadequate for meeting what they consider their basic needs. (These "needs" are usually "wants," not basic needs like food, water, shelter, or warm clothing.)

Talking about the world through the use of maps, globes, and atlases is an effective way of developing global awareness, especially in younger children. Choosing these materials is an important task for parents and educators. It can be a challenging one, as the "shape of the world" is constantly shifting, at least in figurative terms.

Choosing a Map

Any map distorts the shape of the earth. It is impossible to transform a global shape to a flat surface without distorting something: sizes, shapes, directions, or distances between points, for example.

The result of converting the global shape of the earth to a flat surface is called a map projection. There are four basic classifications of map projections: cylindrical, azimuthal, oval, and miscellaneous. Cylindrical projections are rectangular, with latitude and longitude lines shown as a grid of perpendicular lines. Azimuthal projections have a circular outline. Oval projections are, as the name suggests, oval. Miscellaneous projections are those that do not fit into the other categories, such as "interrupted" projections, which look like a segmented orange.

The importance of choosing the right projection for educational purposes cannot be underestimated. There is no one right projection that suits every purpose, but one can narrow the options by considering the purposes for which the map is to be used. When the purpose is the education of young children, accuracy of shape is probably the most important consideration. For older children, who can recognize distortions of shape as such, proportion of sizes is an important consideration.

A poorly chosen map projection can actually be harmful. We tend to believe what we see, and when fundamental geographical relationships... are badly distorted, we are inclined to accept them as fact if we see them that way on maps.... Our mental maps, the brain's geographical "data base," are generated only from what we look at.... A badly distorted map seen regularly (such as one on a television news program backdrop) will look familiar after a while and thus "look right." This can cause one's mental map of the world to become permanently warped.[6]

The most commonly used map projection has been the cylindrical one, probably because it fits better than the other projections do on a rectangular page or poster. The best known cylindrical projection is the Mercator grid (Figure 1), developed by Gerardus Mercator in 1569 and meant to be used as a sailing chart. It greatly exaggerates sizes of countries in the Northern Hemisphere and should not be used as a world map. The Miller cylindrical projection lessens the exaggerations of the Mercator projection, but it does not show correct relative sizes of regions.

The Robinson projection, an oval projection (Figure 2), shows reasonably correct shapes and relative sizes. Distortions occur mostly in the high latitudes in order to show better shapes in the mid- and low-latitude regions. For these reasons, it is recommended for use in educating primary and intermediate level students, who tend to view maps literally.

The Peters projection (Figure 3) is a favorite of justice and peace educators because it shows the correct relative sizes of regions. (Sometimes a Peters projection is printed with a line winding among the continents that divides the First and Third Worlds.)

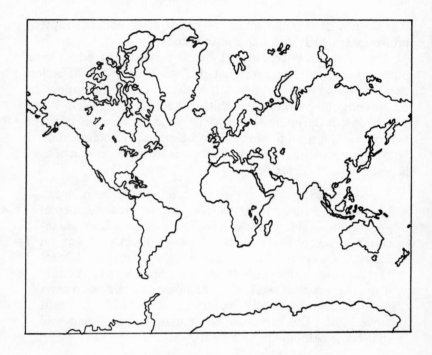

Figure 1. MERCATOR PROJECTION

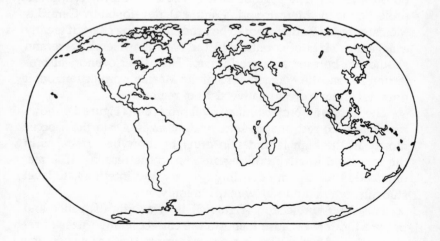

Figure 2. ROBINSON PROJECTION

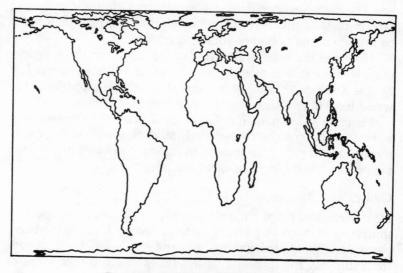

Figure 3. PETERS PROJECTION

This type of cylindrical projection is called "equal area" because it correctly shows the proportional relationship between the sizes of two countries or regions. Its drawback is that it severely distorts the shape of countries. It does correct the Euro-centric bias of maps that make countries in the Northern Hemisphere appear to be larger than those in the Southern Hemisphere. In reality, "the North" is half the size of "the South."

To illustrate this last point, compare the Mercator projection (Figure 1) with the Peters projection (Figure 3). (If you are not sure about national boundaries, you might want to compare map projections that show them.) You will note that on the Mercator map Europe appears to be about the same size as South America. In fact, South America is almost double the size of Europe. The Peters projection shows this fact more accurately. On the Mercator projection, Alaska appears to be larger than Mexico, but the opposite is true. On the Peters projection, Africa is larger than the USSR, which is correct. On the Mercator projection, the USSR is larger. China is four times as large as Greenland, but you wouldn't know that from looking at the Mercator projection, which makes Greenland appear larger. In general, the Mercator projection makes countries in which white people are the majority appear larger than they are. For example, Scandinavia seems larger than India, when, in fact, India is about three times larger.[7] How do these distortions contribute to the notion of white superiority?

How has the exaggerated size of the USSR on the Mercator map, the one that is most familiar to us, contributed to our fear of "the Russians"? What other perceptions of the countries of the world have been shaped by the maps we use?

Hanging a wall map in a classroom or in a child's bedroom, at a level where it can be conveniently studied, is a good beginning for the task of global awareness education — as long as the map projection tells the truth as nearly as possible!

Globes and Atlases

Most elementary-age children enjoy playing with a globe and thumbing through an atlas. Since intermediate level students are particularly good at absorbing facts and figures, they will benefit from studying the facts and figures that accompany the maps of each country in an atlas. A good atlas will contain up-to-date information on the people, politics, economy, and land description for each country. The data on the people of a particular country or region will include population statistics, density, ethnic groups, languages, religions, life expectancy, and literacy rates. The political situation will be described in terms of the type of government, political parties, voting systems, and memberships in international organizations. Discussion of the economy of a country will include its monetary units, per capita income, and information about imports and exports, manufacturing, and agriculture. A world atlas should also provide a physical map for each country, showing such characteristics as mountains, rivers, deserts, and land elevations, as well as a political map, showing boundaries, regions, and cities.

While intermediate students may be interested in these facts and figures for their own sakes, older students can be taught to analyze their meanings. For example, they can learn to draw conclusions about the relationship between per capita income and life expectancy, a basic concept involved in the study of world hunger.

For most effective development of global awareness, an atlas should be used in conjunction with a world map or globe. Children need to think of individual countries in the context of a global setting, not as pages in a fascinating book.

An accurate globe will avoid all the problems of distortion that are characteristics of world maps. However, a globe may not be the most effective educational tool in the home or classroom. Globes are usually expensive, and they tend to become outdated quickly because the world keeps changing! Replacing a map is certainly less costly than replacing a globe. It is also difficult to use a globe as a teaching tool in a classroom full of students. For individual study, though, an up-to-date globe can be very useful.

Summary

Global awareness education aims to teach people how to live in a world that is increasingly interdependent. Global awareness involves an understanding of the peoples, cultures, and resources of the world community. The language we use to talk about the world forms basic impressions of the global environment in which children grow up. Various map projections also contribute to children's understanding of the world. Choosing accurate maps, globes, and atlases is an important task for the parent or educator.

Chapter 3

The Content of
Global Awareness Education

❧

WHAT DO YOU CALL a person who is a citizen of Canada? Of Brazil? Of Nicaragua? Of the United States?

All of these people are Americans. They come from North America, South America, or Central America. When we speak of Americans or the American way of life, however, we are usually referring to the United States. Maybe that's because the word "America" is included in the name of our country. More likely, it's because we've never thought of how citizens of other American countries feel about our claiming exclusively for ourselves a descriptive term that applies to many people beyond our borders. Some of them resent attitudes like this one that ignore their experience.

One aim of global awareness education is to give people the opportunity to stand in one another's shoes so as to experience their lives. In the last chapter, we looked at some basic ways to introduce the concept of global awareness into the everyday consciousness of children. In this chapter, we shall outline the formal content of global awareness education — what information needs to be taught. In the next chapter, we'll examine some attitudes that are also fundamental to building global awareness in children.

Geography: Learning the Facts

Many of us grew up studying a curriculum item called "geography." We learned selective facts and figures about other countries, usually one country at a time, and we drew maps showing rivers, mountains, major cities, and other notable physical characteristics of each country. We might have learned something about the type of government, the major products exported, and the climate.

Even when this information was accurate, it often led to misplaced emphases because it did not raise significant questions that lead to awareness of global perspectives. For example, most of us learned the fact that Great Britain is an island. Very few of us were asked to consider how this fact affects Great Britain's relationship with other European countries. In fact, some British citizens do not consider themselves Europeans because of their separation from the European mainland. This attitude has important implications for the development of a common economic community for Europe, which many of the countries of Europe hope to achieve by 1992. The establishment of a European common market will obviously have an impact on the global economy. The study of geography did not teach us to consider implications such as these of the facts and figures we learned.

In short, we learned information that can be found in an atlas, but we didn't learn much about what it meant in terms of peoples' lives. We didn't learn to think in terms of a global perspective.

It's no secret that students in the United States do poorly on measurements of geographic knowledge, which is fundamental to the development of a global perspective. While there doesn't seem to be any consensus on what to do about this problem, some initiatives have been suggested.

Multicultural or Cross-cultural Education

One approach taken by educators who are concerned about global awareness is to enhance the study of geography by putting some emphasis on cultural regions and peoples. In schools where children of varying ethnic backgrounds are enrolled, efforts are made to celebrate the school's cultural diversity. Children may be given the opportunity to wear "native" dress, to learn some words or phrases in another language and to celebrate cultural holidays by learning songs and dances from another culture and eating ethnic foods. These activities are usually planned as a departure from the daily curriculum, and are therefore "special" events. Often the emphasis is on the differences between U.S. culture and the "foreign" culture. Children usually enjoy these activities, and teachers feel that they are worthwhile because they build an understanding of other cultures.

Such multicultural or cross-cultural educational activities, however, may not contribute significantly to global awareness education. They can too easily become a "tourist" curriculum that leaves students with incomplete or erroneous impressions of what the people of a particular culture are really like. For example, stressing holidays in other cultures may leave children with the impression that people in other cultures spend more time celebrating than going to school or working.

Because multicultural studies tend to stress the differences between cultures, children may not have the opportunity to learn about the daily concerns shared by people everywhere. If multicultural awareness becomes an addition to the curriculum that is treated as a special activity, it does not become a part of the learning atmosphere of a school at the level where values are absorbed and constantly reinforced.

Much of what passes for global awareness education, however well-intentioned, can more accurately be described as multicultural or cross-cultural education. A multicultural or cross-cultural approach to teaching is an updated way of teaching geography, but it is not global awareness education if it does not lead to a global perspective.

Mission Education

Most Christian churches are concerned with evangelizing, with spreading the Gospel to other cultures. Until recently, the goal of evangelization was conversion of "pagan" cultures to Christianity. For some churches, that is still the goal.

The work of most missionaries is no longer described exclusively in such narrow terms. Many missionaries, both lay and religious, witness to the message of the Gospel by joining their lives with those whom they serve. They witness to the Gospel by "doing" it, not just by talking about it. They "walk their talk." They work with the people among whom they live to better their lives through improved educational opportunities, health care, and other development activities. Some groups of people engaged in Christian mission have formed organizations whose primary goal is to assist people in Third World countries with self-determined development needs.[1]

Today, missionaries learn the values of the culture in which they immerse themselves and adapt their own teaching to the culture. No longer do missionaries try to impose Western cultural systems on other cultures. Instead, they seek the common beliefs that varying cultures share and build on them. They bring back to the "mission-sending" country new understandings of values they have learned from so-called mission-receiving countries. In this new understanding of the missionary's role, the "mission-sending" countries also become "mission-receiving" as they learn from other cultures such values as the importance of the extended family, sustainable development techniques, and respect for the natural rhythms of life.

Mission educators contribute to global awareness education when they help us to see ourselves through the eyes of others. From missionaries, we may receive new understandings of our national characteristics that we imagine all people share. For example, African and Asian people will note that people in the United States have a linear view of time: everything is "instant," speed is a value, the future is more important than the past. In other cultures, time is more circular: the rhythms of life repeat themselves, life is experienced as cyclical like the seasons, the present moment is meant to be celebrated, old age is revered. Mission educators can help us learn from the wisdom of other cultures that they have experienced first-hand.

For the most part, mission education focuses on the experiences of particular missionaries in particular places. Because of this focus, it may lack a consistently global perspective. Like multicultural studies, it may contribute to an understanding of other cultures, but may do so in an ethnocentric way. Unlike multicultural studies, it may stress values and beliefs that people share, especially through the practice of religious beliefs.

Because missionaries are often involved in development activities, they can contribute to our understanding of global issues. For example, many missionaries have raised the alarm about environmental concerns because they have seen for themselves the effects of environmental degradation on the people of the Third World.

Development Education

The word "development" is used in such a wide variety of contexts in educational circles that its use in the context of global awareness education requires some definition.

Teachers and parents often think of development in terms of a child's capabilities. We speak of "developmentally appropriate learning activities" when we are involved in curriculum planning.

We want to choose activities that are appropriate to a child's stage of growth.

Economists think of development in terms of economic capabilities. We have already discussed the categorizing of countries as "more developed" or "less developed" in those terms. In this scheme of things, the goals of development are industrialization and economic self-sufficiency. Education for this kind of development does not necessarily contribute to global awareness.

Development education that contributes to global awareness has to do with the dissemination of facts about Third World countries and their economic, social, and political problems. It puts this information in a global perspective in such a way that the learner can recognize issues of justice. The goal of development education in this context is to move people to action and advocacy on behalf of the needs of people in the Third World.

Development education may include limited examination of structural inequities that cause problems. However, most development education programs concentrate on providing factual information about the Third World in such a way that people in the United States will understand how their lifestyles affect people in the Third World. Development education teaches the realities of interdependence.

Development Issues

In the context of the social studies curriculum in the classroom or discussion around the dinner table at home, development education deals with the specific social, economic, and political issues of survival and growth that affect all people, but particularly people in the Third World in an immediate way. Here is a survey of some of those issues, along with considerations that enter into the discussion. We shall examine some of these issues in more detail in later chapters.

Hunger. World hunger is one of the most common starting points in development education. Even the youngest child is aware that somewhere in the world people are starving. In cities throughout the United States, people of all ages line up at soup kitchens to be fed. No longer is hunger a problem that we see only on the evening news. For most of us, evidence of the problem of hunger is right in our own back yards.

Some people think that people are hungry because they are

too lazy to work to earn their food or because they refuse to give up inefficient methods of farming even in the face of a dwindling food supply. Other people argue that there is plenty of food to feed everyone in the world, but maldistribution problems are the reason that people are starving. These people regard food as a basic human right to which everyone is entitled, not as an economic commodity. They argue that the problem can be traced to political systems that allow people to starve even when there is food available.

Population. Related to the problem of food shortages is the issue of overpopulation. Some people believe that people in Third World countries don't have enough to eat because they have too many mouths to feed. They believe that the problem of hunger could be solved if people didn't have so many children. Others argue that poor parents will continue to bear children so long as child mortality rates are high in order to have more hands to help support their families, particularly when the parents grow too old to take care of themselves. Religious beliefs about the morality of birth control also play a part in the discussion.

The Environment. As awareness of the vulnerability of the natural resources of our planet grows, so does awareness of our interdependence with one another. We may be concerned with such local problems as the growing size of our landfills and the hazards of toxic waste, but we cannot escape the fact that such problems as acid rain, the pollution of the oceans, the depletion of the ozone layer and changes in the atmosphere are global in scope.

So-called green movements around the world are made up of activists who challenge the goals of economic development when they deplete the earth's resources. These environmentalists argue for sustainable development, "development that meets the needs of the present without compromising the ability of future generations to meet their own needs."[2]

In the Third World, indigenous peoples have been driven off their lands and forced to abandon their traditional practices of sustainable use of resources, to the detriment of the environment, by the demands of technological progress. Landless people in Third World countries cannot afford to take a long-range view of environmental needs when they are struggling for survival, so they use agricultural methods that produce immediate results, such as "slash-and-burn" farming. Each planting season, forests are destroyed so that crops may be grown. When the soil is worn out the farmer moves on. Poverty and the degradation of the environment are inextricably related.

Urbanization. When land cannot support agriculture, or when most of the fertile land is held by a few wealthy landowners, subsistence farmers will migrate to cities in search of employment. Often they leave their families behind in rural villages, in effect making women heads of households. Most cities in Third World countries cannot sustain this influx. Slums spring up, further degrading the urban environment. Rivers become polluted due to increased industrialization and lack of sanitation facilities, causing problems for people who live downstream.

In 1960, Mexico City had a population of about ten million. By the year 2000, the population will probably reach thirty-one million. Other cities in Third World countries are experiencing similar growth. At the same time, a study of eighty-three countries revealed that 3 percent of the landowners controlled 80 percent of the land. It should be obvious that land reform is one answer to the problems of urbanization.[3]

Women in Development. Women bear much of the burden of development in the Third World, but their work is frequently overlooked by development planners. Women grow and prepare food, an arduous daily responsibility that may include the search for firewood and clean water. A CARE study found that women in rural Kenya who are heads of households spend 50 percent of their work time collecting water and 17 percent of their time preparing food. Often they must boil the water to make it safe, which means using scarce fuel.[4]

Cultural and religious inhibitions may bar women from education, even basic education about simple hygiene, health care, or improved agricultural techniques. Like their sisters in the First World, women in the Third World who do find employment earn much less than men do.

Disarmament. In 1989, the U.S. government sent Third World nations $9.3 billion in arms and military aid compared to $5.9 billion in development and food aid.[5] Advocates of disarmament claim that providing military assistance to Third World countries not only depletes our own financial resources and deprives people in need of food and development aid, it also helps to fuel ongoing conflicts in nations that can ill afford to be at war. Others argue that

Third World nations are in danger of being taken over by Marxist governments if they do not receive U.S. military assistance.

Literacy. Almost 900,000,000 people in the world cannot read and write. That's nine hundred million. In ten countries, most of them in Africa, four out of five children are not in school, either because the government does not provide schools or because the children are needed at home to help provide for family needs. To bring the world's population of children up to the level of attendance in First World countries, an additional 230 million children would need to be enrolled. The cost would amount to less than $50 billion, one-third the amount that Third World countries are spending for military needs. Yet illiteracy can be overcome if nations are willing to put "mind" over "military."[6] The people of Sri Lanka, for example, have achieved an 85 percent literacy rate, as compared with an average of 45 percent for countries with similar per capita incomes, because they chose to concentrate their limited economic resources on primary education rather than on other priorities.[7]

The list of topics could go on. Development education deals with any topic that has to do with the way distribution of resources affects human survival. The goal of development education is to inform the learner with an understanding that improving the quality of life for impoverished people is a global process that involves action and advocacy on their behalf as well as an examination of the impact of First World lifestyles on Third World lives.

Justice and Peace Education

Justice and peace education is an ongoing process that enables the learner to value the dignity of the individual, to recognize the interdependence of all human beings, to act responsibly, to recognize oppression, and to participate in actions that promote cooperation and correct injustices.

Very few educators and parents would deny that justice and peace education is an integral part of global awareness education. The problem is that not everyone can agree on a definition of justice.

Many citizens of the United States understand justice in terms of equality. We speak of "equal opportunity" in employment when we mean that everyone has the same right to be considered for a position. Proponents of capital punishment make the case that a person who takes a life must pay with a life: one life equals one life.

Children think of justice in terms of what is "fair." If one child in a group receives more of something desirable than the other children in the group, someone will inevitably pipe up, "That's not fair." Younger children will frequently argue with parents or teachers that older children have more privileges and "that's not fair." Teenagers who are not permitted the same privileges as their peers, even though "everyone else is allowed to," will argue that parents are being unfair.

One of the most valuable lessons we can teach our children is that life isn't fair. Ask any Third World child whose belly is distended with malnutrition how "fair" life is. We cannot make life "fair," nor should we. We cannot make life's opportunities equal for everyone, nor should we. (Every teenager does not need the opportunity to own or drive an automobile — or to have a job to pay for the expenses of maintaining a vehicle for personal use.) We can, however, do justice for everyone — and we should.

Justice requires that we recognize that all people have certain fundamental rights: to life, to food, to shelter, to adequate medical care, to education, to employment, to clean air and water, to physical and emotional security, to participation in the processes that govern their lives. Justice requires that we work to achieve those rights for every human being.

Justice is concerned with establishing right relationships between nations and peoples and with nurturing the harmonious relationship of human beings with the earth for the sake of generations to come. Justice does not have to do with providing opportunities for accumulating goods or privileges. A justice perspective promotes the concept of interdependence, the understanding that all human beings are linked to one another because of our common humanity and that we are responsible for the consequences of our actions as they affect other people. Justice requires, for example, that we "live simply so that others may simply live." Justice recognizes that economic development alone does not meet the needs of human development. Justice leads people to recognize the need for solidarity.

A story from the Philippines tells the meaning of justice better than any definition. It concerns the principle of *damayan*. According to this principle, each person's resources and needs are shared by the local community. Hunger is shared, and so are surpluses. In the village of Pampanga, when a farmer had to take his daughter to a hospital in Manila, his neighbors tended his fields, without payment, so that he would not lose his rice crop, his means of livelihood. The farmer received what he needed from his neighbors without any expectation that he would repay them. There was nothing "fair" about this arrangement, but justice was done.[8]

Jesus told a similar story, which we call the parable of the laborers in the vineyard (Matt. 20:1–16). This parable is about justice, and people always have a lot of trouble with it. You know the story: workers are called to the vineyard at various hours of the day. At the end of the day, they are all paid a full day's wage, even those who worked the least amount of time. The listener cannot help but react "that's not fair." It isn't fair, but it is just. Those who worked a full day received the agreed-upon wage. They were not cheated in any way. Those who worked only part-time received what they needed: a day's wage. We don't know why the latecomers were late, but that isn't important. What is important is that their basic needs were met.

A justice and peace perspective in education teaches children to ask why basic needs are not met and to strategize about what can be done to correct injustice. Until they reach junior high level, children will probably not be able to identify the elements of systemic injustice without help, but they can be taught to recognize cause and effect scenarios once they are explained.

Even very young children can be taught to recognize the effects their actions have on others and to modify their behavior (most of the time!). When children are systematically taught to look beyond the parameters of their own lives, they begin to acquire a global consciousness.

A Comprehensive Definition

What, then, is global awareness education? Various educators will supply different definitions depending on the values and purposes of global awareness that they endorse. However, there are some elements that should be common to any definition of the purpose of global awareness education:

- an appreciation of both the diversity and the common humanity of the people and cultures of the world;

- an awareness of the tensions between national self-interest and global responsibility;

- a knowledge of basic facts about geography and development issues;

- an understanding of basic human rights;

- an understanding of justice as right relationship that leads to peace among human beings;

- a grasp of skills needed to promote action and advocacy that lead to an enhanced quality of life for all oppressed people, especially those in the Third World.

Effective global awareness education leads to informed advocacy and action. It is a gradual process that begins in infancy. It never ends.

Summary

There is no generally recognized consensus about what constitutes global awareness education. Multicultural, or cross-cultural, studies focus on particular regions or peoples, but they lack a global perspective. Mission education may contribute to global awareness education when it stresses values and beliefs that people in different parts of the world share. Missionaries may also contribute to our understanding of global awareness through their direct involvement in development issues.

Development education that contributes to global awareness has to do with the dissemination of facts about Third World countries and their economic, social, and political problems. Development education with a justice and peace perspective helps learners to recognize systemic global problems and to take action to improve the quality of life for oppressed peoples. Effective global awareness education is an ongoing process that leads to informed advocacy and action.

Chapter 4

Valuing Differences, Making Connections: Attitudes That Promote Global Awareness

~

IMAGINE WHAT THE WORLD would be like if people looked the same, had the same abilities, held the same values, and were interested in the same things. Boring, you would immediately say — because that's what you've been taught to say. If we really believed that, though, I wouldn't be writing this chapter, and discrimination would be only a word in the dictionary.

One of the most prevalent myths in the culture of the United States is that our nation is a melting pot. The metaphor suggests a national portrait composed of the best of each culture represented in our national makeup. A tour of most cities in the United States would paint a different picture. We are more like a mosaic made up of different colors and shapes and values and beliefs, or a bouquet composed of many different blossoms.

Not all of us are comfortable with that image. We prefer to think that "real Americans" are white persons of European descent — and the longer the line of descent, the more "American," so long as it doesn't go back to native Americans.

American history didn't begin with European voyages of discovery. Indigenous Amerindians discovered Columbus as much as Columbus discovered them. A significant task that global awareness educators in the United States face is to get children to stop believing in a hierarchy of values that automatically puts European culture at the top.[1]

Original Sin and Global Awareness

According to the literal interpretation of Genesis, the origins of human evil had something to do with snacking on an apple. The myth is not about hunger for food; it's about hunger for power. The original sin was wanting to be like God, wanting to shape others in our own image.

We seek assurance of our own worth in the likeness of others. People who are like us in appearance, beliefs, and values validate the worth of our own identities. People who are different threaten our identities, our choices, our way of life. So we clothe ourselves, with determination, in our own point of view to hide our nakedness and vulnerability from one another, as Adam and Eve did.

"In the end," according to one educator, "we will conserve only what we love; we will love only what we understand; we will understand only what we are taught."[2] One role of global awareness educators is to teach the kind of understanding that leads children to care about all the peoples of the earth.

We can teach children about other cultures in order to satisfy their curiosity, in which case people of different cultures will be known as interesting "others." Or we can teach them the need to learn about other cultures so that we can compete in a global economy, a motivation derived from the need to control the dynamics of global interaction. Better by far to teach children about other cultures so that they can understand and accept diversity without making preconceived value judgments and so that they can make connections between their lives and the lives of people who seem "different."

To know and be known by the other was God's original plan for human relationship. In humanitarian terms, unity is the potential toward which we strive for personal fulfillment. In global awareness terms, the task of the educator is to teach students to make connections with other cultures so that they can literally "stand in the shoes" of people they have not met.

In the United States today, we are becoming more and more aware of the cultural diversity of our citizens. Unfortunately, we don't all value that diversity. Racial and ethnic tensions are increasing. Yesterday's "melting pot" has become today's "pressure cooker." Differences in gender, ethnicity, race, and age are causes for divisions. These have "an inevitable trickle-down effect on children."[3]

Different Does Not Mean Bad

Acceptance of individual differences begins in the home and in the classroom. Children — and adults — have the tendency to think that family members and close friends will share their understandings of situations and agree with their opinions just because they are family or friends. In some marriages, there is an unwritten expectation that spouses will never disagree with one another's opinions — at least in public. Educating for global awareness begins with the recognition that "different" does not mean "bad."

Every psychologically healthy individual has preferred ways of viewing the world, gathering and processing information, and making decisions about that information. Children are no exception. Adults who respect children's preferences, even when they don't share them, are teaching children that differences among people are part of the wonderful diversity of the human family.

Understanding Each Other

A theory of personality type developed by psychologist Carl Jung[4] and adapted by Katharine Briggs and her daughter Isabel Briggs Myers has been widely used since the Myers-Briggs Type Indicator (MBTI) was developed in the 1960s. Type theory tries to explain human behavior in terms of individual preferences for interacting with others, gathering information, and making decisions.

Efforts to explain human behavior in terms of personality theory go back to Hippocrates. Such theories help us to value the differences in one another, to avoid the "original sin" of trying to create others in our own image. Type theory is especially useful in marriage counseling and in helping co-workers understand one another's preferred work styles. It is not meant to diagnose personality disorders or even to describe a person's aptitudes. It simply indicates preferred ways of behaving. Individuals may be perfectly capable of behaving in a number of the ways suggested by type theory, but they usually choose a preferred way.

The MBTI divides people up into one of sixteen personality types, all of them good. (Types indicate preferences between "good" ways of interacting with the world, not "good" or "bad" ways of relating. In the MBTI scheme of things, all differences are good.) Of course, we might have reason to be skeptical of any system that divides the world's population into only sixteen categories. However, type theory is a useful corrective to the idea that there is one "right" way to do or to see things. Parents and teachers familiar with type theory can understand different learning styles among children and help to structure learning situations to suit a child's preferences.

A person's type is reported by four letters that represent preferences between two possibilities in each of four areas of personality style. Individuals don't make these choices consciously. Preferences simply reflect the way an individual uses personal energy most comfortably.

According to the theory, an individual is either an Extravert (E) or an Introvert (I). These letters represent a person's basic attitude toward the world. Extraverts learn by interacting with others. They need to "think out loud" in order to draw conclusions. They can "think on their feet" and are quick to answer questions. It's sometimes hard to know what an extravert really means, since the learning process is going on as he or she talks. Introverts, on the other hand, prefer to work things out in their heads before speaking. Introverts do not like to be asked to say what they think until they are ready to speak. They need time to process information. "Talking things out" energizes extraverts and exhausts introverts.

When it comes to gathering information, individuals prefer either the Sensing (S) function or the Intuitive (N) function. ("N" is used to refer to intuition, since "I" denotes the introvert.) Sensing types, as might be expected, use their senses to gather information. They are attentive to detail, and they like to deal in specifics. Intuitive types prefer to look for relationships and possibilities. They focus on the "big picture." They are dreamers and are quickly bored by routine. S people have a problem with N people because N types don't pay attention to detail and they often generalize without reference to specifics. N people may regard S people as nit-pickers who lack vision. In the classroom, S students prefer multiple-choice tests; N students prefer essays.

The decision-making function is designated by the letters T or F. Making decisions is a matter of logic for Thinking (T) types. What is important to the T type is whether something is true or false. T types understand cause and effect, and they like to stick to principles. They are good at analysis. Feeling (F) types are more concerned with relationships. They may decide things by making comparisons or associations. They value the feelings of other people and they do not like conflict. In a group situation, preserving harmony is so important to F types that they will avoid confrontation.

In my experience, the differences between the preferences of Thinking and Feeling types cause the most misunderstandings. T types can be inflexible about acknowledging that different values can shape decisions. They are convinced that logic is the only valid basis for making reasonable decisions. F types can consider T types rigid and legalistic, while T types may consider F types emotional and irrational. F types can tolerate differences of opinion for the sake of preserving harmony. They can irritate T types by refusing to face up to problems caused by differences of opinion. Parents and teachers who prefer the T process for making decisions need to be sensitive to the perspective of children who prefer the F process — and vice versa.

The final attitude in the profile is either Judging (J) or Perceiving (P). These indicate preferences for processing and prioritizing information and for coming to closure on questions or projects. The person who prefers the J attitude likes to proceed in an orderly fashion, preferably with schedules or agendas. The J type likes to "get going" on a project as soon as it's assigned and to finish it quickly. The J type can be in such a hurry that decisions are made without enough information. The P type, on the other hand, hates to make decisions because he or she never has enough information. Perceivers like spontaneity and can tolerate ambiguity well since they are open-minded. They tend to procrastinate and they can appear disorganized, which is annoying to J types.

Personality types can usually be determined with some accuracy by applying descriptions such as the ones just given to observation of an individual's behavior. The type is reported as four letters. For example, the most common type in the United States is ESTJ. The first and last letters indicate attitudes; the second and third letters indicate mental functions.

The MBTI itself is a written inventory of preferences that the individual chooses to produce the profile of his or her type. The MBTI is designed to be administered and scored by qualified personnel. A self-scoring type inventory, the Keirsey Temperament Sorter, is also available.[5]

According to type theory, infants and young children have "undifferentiated" personalities. They have no preferences. Children between the ages of six and twelve develop a preference for one of the four functions (S, N, T, or F), which is referred to as the "dominant" function. In adolescence they begin to develop their "second favorite," or "auxiliary" function.[6] (If S or N is the dominant function, then T or F will be the auxiliary. If T or F is dominant, then S or N will be auxiliary. Remember that opposite functions cannot operate at the same time. The choice is between S and N and between T and F.) The alert teacher or parent will take these preferences into account in designing teaching strategies.

Children won't derive much benefit from explanations of type theory, but they will benefit from understanding that personality differences are not bad. Understanding these differences can give children an appreciation of their own strengths as well as of the gifts and talents of other children. For example, the "shy" child may simply be an introvert who needs time to process information. The child who is always talking in class is probably an extravert who needs to talk in order to learn. The extravert can keep a discussion going. The introvert, who may appear to be uninvolved, may offer the most constructive conclusions. Parents and teachers who recognize and draw on these possibilities affirm the differences in children's personalities.

For adults, an introduction to type theory can be an eye-opener, particularly when it explains perceived personality conflicts. Some adults, particularly T types, won't find much value in it because it doesn't "prove" anything. The brief outline given here hardly does justice to the possibilities for applications of type theory to group dynamics and conflict resolution.

From an educational point of view, type theory is a useful tool both for teaching tolerance of differing viewpoints and for recognizing differences in learning styles. When parents and teachers respect and value differences in personality and learning styles in children, they teach children that diversity enriches human society.

Dealing with Discrimination

Children may not pay much attention to personality differences among themselves. They do, however, pay attention to physical differences. Impressions of such differences are formed early, and attitudes toward physical differences are quickly learned from adults. According to Louise Derman-Sparks, who is actively involved in anti-bias education, "Much learning occurs spontaneously and informally, when adults respond to children's comments and behaviors."[7]

The damage done to children who suffer from discrimination because of gender, color, race, or physical disability hardly needs description. Parents and teachers know from experience that children, even young children, can be cruel and that they will use stereotypes to disparage one another when they are angry or upset. ("You can't climb high because you're a girl." "I don't want to hold your hand; it's dirty because it's brown." "You can't play ball because you can't run in a wheelchair.") A child exposed to these messages with any frequency will surely suffer diminished self-esteem and self-confidence.

The child who learns that discriminatory behavior is acceptable will also suffer. Biased behavior is a result of an individual's need to control others, either because of fear of the other or because of lack of self-esteem. The child who is allowed or even encouraged to learn biased attitudes toward others will develop a false sense of superiority. He or she will acquire an attitude of privilege that leads to expectations of preferred treatment because of gender or color or physical abilities. While some institutions in our society do support such expectations, a child who grows up with such expectations will be ill-equipped to live in a society characterized by cultural pluralism.

Children begin to notice differing physical characteristics at an early age. Gender is usually the first difference that two-year-olds notice. Awareness of diversity in skin color also occurs about this time, when children start to learn the names of colors. They notice distinctions in hair texture, such as coarse, fine, curly, or straight. Awareness of physical disabilities begins a little later. Before they are three, children recognize cultural aspects of gender and ethnic identity, as, for example, household roles assigned by gender. By the age of five, children have usually interiorized the norms, stereotypes, and biases of their social setting.[8]

Children will generalize in their own minds about the differences they note. They may not verbalize their assumptions. Silence does not mean that a child takes no notice of differences.

Research has shown that active intervention by parents and teachers is necessary if children are to become comfortable with people of different races or physical abilities. Simply exposing children to children of other backgrounds isn't sufficient. Children who are confused by differences may feel mildly uncomfortable. It's not the differences that cause the problem; it's the way children react to them that may create bias.[9]

Parents and teachers need to allow children to make note of differences and to talk about them. Adults will need to be sensitive to the "body language" of children who don't voice discomfort, e.g., a white child who consistently moves away from brown-skinned or Asian children, or a child who avoids children with disabilities. Consciously or unconsciously, the child who exhibits these behaviors is evaluating the other children as undesirable.

Children need accurate feedback about the differences they notice so that they won't develop prejudices. Telling a child that "we're all the same," or that it's not polite to discuss skin color or disabilities, doesn't help. Children's questions, both asked and unasked, need to be answered simply and directly as appropriate occasions arise. Children who exhibit biased behavior need to be corrected gently but firmly without delay. Children need to know that belittling someone else's identity is unacceptable behavior.

Left unexamined, children's assumptions about gender or ethnic differences may grow into stereotypes. Many stereotypes do have some foundation in experience. Stereotypes develop when limited experience of one individual or situation is generalized to apply to larger groups or situations of which the learner has little or no experience. ("Cindy likes to play with dolls. All girls like to play with dolls." "Remi is a good dancer. All blacks are good dancers.") Adults may introduce or perpetuate such stereotypes by voicing their own unexamined biases.

Prejudices, or negative biases, are a defense mechanism of insecure children — and insecure adults. They develop in individuals who are not sure of or satisfied with their own identities or who perceive differences as threats to their well-being. Children who have confidence in their own identities and abilities do not need to disparage other children in order to feel powerful. The same is true for adults.

Making Connections

Terry, my co-worker, was reviewing a video sent to us by a missionary in Tanzania who works among the Masai people. Nick, her four-year-old, watched the footage with fascination. He noted the unfamiliar garb the people were wearing, the way they used gourds to milk cows and feed infants, and the different sounds of their language. But he also noted something that was familiar to him: "Listen, Mom, the cows are mooing in English."

One of the developmental tasks of children is to learn the meanings of "same" and "different." Obvious differences are easy for children to spot. Intermediate and junior high students are fascinated by cultural differences, especially if they are perceived as bizarre or exotic. Recognizing similarities isn't always so easy, especially similarities that people of all cultures share. Even when common ground is recognized, it may be labeled in First World terms — like Nick's assumption about the language cows speak.

A good place to start recognizing similarities between people is with the emotional needs that all humans share. Children, perhaps better than adults, understand the need to be loved. They know what it means to want to be safe from harm. They can recognize oppression when they have to live with arbitrary rules they don't understand. They know how it feels to be "left out" for no good reason.

Children can also be taught to recognize fundamental physical needs — for food, for shelter, for adequate medical care. They can recognize the need for education, even if they don't like school!

Recognizing basic human needs requires that children be able to distinguish needs from "wants." Children in First World countries often take the fulfillment of basic needs for granted, to the point that they think of them as rights to which they're entitled. That assumption is correct. What children need to understand is that they are entitled to the fulfillment of basic human needs because they are human beings and not just because they are citizens of the First World. The same rights they enjoy also belong to all the children of the world.

On November 20, 1989, the United Nations adopted by consensus the first international convention (binding agreement) on children's rights after ten years of negotiation among member countries. The agreement recognizes "the right of every child to a standard of living adequate for the child's physical, mental, spiritual, moral and social development" (Article 27). Among other rights, these include the right to adequate nutrition and health care; clothing; shelter; education; national identity; nondiscrimination; freedom of thought, conscience, and religion; and the right to play and recreation. This last-named right is a recognition that play is fundamental to a child's development; it is the "work" of children.

The preamble to the convention recognizes that "the child, for the full and harmonious development of his or her personality, should grow up in a family environment, in an atmosphere of happiness, love and understanding." It also notes that "in all countries in the world there are children living in exceptionally difficult conditions, and that such children need special consideration."[10]

Children who have never been deprived of their basic needs may have a hard time imagining what it would be like to go hungry or homeless, or to be deprived of educational opportunities even at the primary level, or to be removed from their family environment, or to be forced to go to work at a very young age. They need to be made aware that some children do suffer from these deprivations. They need to be able to imagine how it would feel to "walk in the shoes" of deprived children or, more accurately, to walk in the footsteps of children who lack even shoes.

Focusing on the rights that all children share is one way to develop a sense of common ground among children. The right to play should provoke interesting discussions! Creating awareness of the deprivation of fundamental rights can evoke compassion for the less fortunate in children who enjoy those rights. For older children, this awareness could lead to an examination of social and political structures that deprive children of their rights. Understanding the effects of deprivation can also teach children (and adults) not to judge the capabilities and efforts of other people without considering the resources available to them.

Simulation games are effective teaching devices for stimulating awareness of deprivation of rights. Even young children can learn from simple simulations. I once asked a group of second-graders to fast from after-school snacks and dinner before coming to an evening lesson on hunger awareness. Without any prompting, the children described the effects of hunger on their daily activities: "I was a grouch." "I couldn't do my homework or learn anything because I was so hungry." "I didn't want to play; I didn't have enough energy." Children who can reflect on such experiences will think twice before making any assumptions about the intellectual or social capacities of hungry people.

Talking about deprivation of individual rights is effective. Talking about deprivation of rights that affects the family is even more productive since it develops the concept of the interdependence of systems. For example, children can see that discrimination against a parent also affects a child when it deprives the parent of the means for providing for children's needs. (Children depend on parents, who depend on employers or on the economic system to provide opportunities for meaningful work.) Depriving children of the opportunity for education limits the economic potential of children's ability to care for their parents in their old age. (Parents depend on the state to provide an educational system for children so that children can grow into adults capable of caring for themselves and for their elderly parents.)

Teaching human rights from a family-centered perspective also allows children to see the diversity of family structures. Children should consider the rights of all kinds of families: two-parent families, one-parent families, extended families, two-earner families, families where one or both parents are unemployed, families in which someone is chronically ill or disabled, multiracial families and so on. What rights do families have based on special needs? Here is one instance where the distinction between "fairness" and "justice" may prove instructive! By extension, the question of the rights of systematically deprived people in Third World countries can then be posed.

The ability to understand concepts such as justice depends on the ability to make connections. Just as global awareness education requires that we teach children to value diversity, it also requires that we teach them to make connections and to recognize similarities. Making connections between their own feelings, needs, and experiences and the lives of other children is one way to develop compassion and empathy in the children we teach. Both words have their root meanings in "being with" others, and both attitudes lead to action on behalf of the dispossessed.

Moving from compassion aroused by awareness of a human rights problem to recognition that poverty is a structural problem is part of the developmental process of global awareness education. Seven-year-olds can recognize the effects of hunger and empathize with the plight of hungry children, but they may not be able to understand the reasons why people are chronically hungry. Adolescents can understand and examine the economic, social, and political systems that contribute to the problem, at least in a general way.

As awareness of the complexity and enormity of the problem grows, all of us should grow too in humility and in respect for the poor of the world, who know their own needs and remain hopeful about their own capacities to solve their problems in the face of unrelenting poverty. From their needs, we in the First World can learn the true meaning of need and how to live without "wants" that we don't need.

Summary

Global awareness education entails the formation of attitudes that promote understanding among people. Learning to value diversity in individual personalities and in gender, color, race, and physical ability is important for parents and teachers as well as for children.

Children develop biases early, and they learn from imitation. Parents and teachers need to intervene actively to teach children to be comfortable with people who are perceived as "different." Children need to be taught that "different" isn't "bad."

Parents and teachers who understand a child's preferred methods of gathering, organizing, and evaluating information will be able to construct effective learning strategies and will also demonstrate to the child that diverse styles of interaction make human activity interesting. People do not have to think and act alike in order to be right about ideas or ways of doing things.

Children also need to learn to make connections between their experiences and those of other people. The capacity to make connections and to understand the concept of interdependence is necessary for developing a sense of justice. One way that children can make connections is to learn and discuss the needs and rights that all children share by virtue of their common humanity.

People in the First World can learn from people in the Third World the difference between "needs" and "wants." Global awareness education should lead to attitudes of empathy and compassion that promote action on behalf of justice.

Chapter 5

How Children Learn

~

A<small>S A YOUNG CHILD</small>, one of my cousins was convinced that bananas grew on top of refrigerators (or "iceboxes," as they were called in our extended family). He had no reason to think otherwise. His mother, my mother, and our other aunt all kept them there. A child checking on the availability of bananas in any of the three households always knew where to look. Our family grew bananas on refrigerator tops.

This same cousin's mother has a zany sense of humor. When I was about five, she and I were sharing a slice of watermelon one day. I asked her what would happen if I swallowed one of the seeds. By way of an answer, she swallowed one, walked out of the room and returned a moment later with a sprig of ivy trailing out of her ear. Once I recovered from my astonishment, she showed me that she was joking. Even though she assured me that swallowing watermelon seeds will not cause greenery to grow out of my ear, I have never swallowed one since that day. The experience of seeing ivy "grow" out of my aunt's ear made a lasting impression on me. As the old saying goes, "seeing is believing," even when what we see is an illusion.

How Do You Know?

My cousin and I both drew some conclusions based on what we observed with our eyes. If we had had more information or more experience of the origins of bananas and watermelons, we might have drawn different conclusions.

The process by which children discover and learn to relate to the realities of the world around them is not easy to study or to define because children are not able to articulate abstract ideas in a scientific way. Most of what we know about the ways children learn comes from observing them in various learning environments.

Educators have proposed a number of theories of learning. Some of these enjoy more credibility than others for reasons having more to do with the mechanics of classroom management than with the learning capacities of children. Given the state of education in the United States today, it seems safe to say that no one has yet developed a comprehensive theory of how children learn that has proven itself effective in classrooms.

In this chapter, we shall briefly survey basic learning theories as they apply to children. We'll look at two types of learning: how children acquire knowledge of the physical world around them and how they learn moral values. Much of the literature on these theories is loaded with jargon and is not easy to interpret. My purpose here is not to interpret or comment on the theories, but simply to describe them as I understand them. With that foundation, I'll add my own unscientific observations of how children — and adults — learn, based on my experience as a parent and as an educator.

If you are a parent or teacher who is reasonably conversant with current educational theory, or if you don't find much value in unscientific observations, you might want to skip this chapter. If, like me, you have found that educational theories and methods you have learned don't always seem to apply very well to your own children or to the children you teach, read on.

Left Out by Language

First, a joke about jargon. This one is based on the passage in the Gospels where Jesus asks his disciples who people think he is. The joke made the rounds of religious educators a few years ago; it goes like this:

> And Jesus said unto them, "Who do you say that I am?" And they replied, "You are the eschatological manifestation of the ground of our being, the kerygma in which we can find the ultimate meaning of our interpersonal relationships." And Jesus said, "What?"

I have the same reaction when I study educational theory, which I seldom do because I find it too jargon-laden and theoretical. I am grateful to those who seek to understand and explain to the rest of us how the minds of children work, so that we might lead them to the development of their best human potential, but

I often have a hard time drawing practical applications from their conclusions.

I am convinced that many parents and teachers are so intimidated by the complexity of educational theories that they do not trust their own instincts and basic common sense when it comes to teaching the children for whom they are responsible. The result is that parents, in particular, lack confidence about their role as their children's most influential teachers. (One of the most frustrating questions that parents pose to teachers is "Why didn't my child learn such-and-such?" The correct answer from the teachers is "Because you didn't teach it to her.")

Most parents know more about how children learn and what they need to learn than they think they do. So do most teachers. Both parents and teachers who work directly with children need to claim some autonomy in teaching situations. School boards and curriculum specialists should not be the sole decision-makers about either the content or the method of children's education.

Basics of Learning Theory

There are two poles of thought as to how children learn. In popular parlance, we call this the "nature vs. nurture" controversy. Some theorists say that children are born with knowledge that emerges in a predictable sequence of steps as they mature. This is the "nature" school of thought. Others have theorized that children's minds are blank slates when they are born and that they learn what is taught from "outside" themselves by their interaction with the environment and by those who teach and care for them. These differing points of view are also described in terms of "heredity" versus "environment," especially when the discussion is about factors that influence learning.

Few educational theorists would adhere strictly to one pole or the other. Most people can agree that children do seem to "know" some things without having them formally taught. The same people would agree that children are not born "knowing" the names of the countries of the world. These have to be learned. The issue is not really whether or not the child is born with the capacity to learn this information. The issue for most educators is how the information should be taught.

The "empiricist" school of thought holds that children learn through what is experienced by the senses. Knowledge is external to the child and is internalized through the senses. "Rationalists" agree that sensory experience is important to learning, but they point out that some things cannot be learned by the use of the senses because they are not available to sensory experience. For example, the innate power of reason is necessary for learning truths that cannot be observed, like the laws of mathematics. Children may hear the operations of arithmetic explained by a teacher, or observe them by seeing them written out on a chalkboard, but they need the power of reason to make the logical connections by which they can "figure out" arithmetic problems.

As is the case with most conflicting theories, the truth is probably larger than either of these theories and somewhere in the realm where the two might converge. A third theory, proposed by Jean Piaget, is called the "constructivist" approach. It endorses neither the rationalist nor the empiricist approach, but finds elements of truth in both of them. For Piaget, knowledge is acquired by the child's interaction with the environment. The child has an innate capacity to construct meaning out of this interaction by making connections between objects. The child can then "construct" relationships between objects. For example, the child can describe objects as "the same" or "different." The problem here, which Piaget recognized, is that children may not have enough information or experience to describe relationships accurately. Piaget maintained that reason is not innate, but is the result of the child's creation.[1]

Implications for the Educational Setting

Most of our school systems are based on the empiricist approach to knowledge. Children's minds are assumed to be empty vessels into which the teachers pour knowledge. At each grade level, teachers fill the vessels to a predetermined point with a specific body of knowledge before they "pass" them on to the next grade level. This is probably less a reflection of adherence to theory than it is a reflection of economic realities. There is little question of the value of individualized learning that structures the context of meaningful experiences for students according to their own interests and readiness. These experiences provide the motivation that stimulates learning from "inside" the student. However, such methods require time, energy, funding, and opportunities that are usually not available to the average teacher.

As an example of the dilemma of structuring a method of instruction that works best, let's take another look at how my cousin might have learned about the origin of bananas. His original observation, made by the use of his sight, was that bananas can be found on the tops of refrigerators. Since he observed this phenomenon in more than one location, he reasoned that this was true in all locations. (Most young children lack a perspective that extends much beyond their immediate environment, so this wasn't an unreasonable assumption for him to make at his age.) Had he had the opportunity to make a trip to the grocery store, or had he seen bananas growing on trees, he could have made other, more accurate assumptions. Theoretically, the best method of instruction would be to provide him with those experiences. However, we all know that it's impossible to take a group of preschoolers on a trip to the tropics so that they can see bananas in their native setting. The time and expense involved would be prohibitive — not to mention the logistical details of organizing a group of five-year-olds for such an excursion. Besides, a curriculum composed of nothing but such "experiences" would quickly degenerate into chaos, except in the hands of the most skillful and creative teachers working with small groups of highly motivated students. Such a structure simply isn't possible for most school systems. Much of the attraction of private schools is that they usually offer some "enrichment" possibilities along these lines.

I imagine my cousin learned the truth about bananas the way most people do. Someone told him.

Developmental Theory

One of the most important roles of educators, be they parents or teachers, is to provide children with experiences that help them to develop accurate understandings of the world around them. According to the theories of developmental psychologists, these experiences should be appropriate to the child's capabilities and aptitudes at a given age.

"Developmental" theory holds that a child's capabilities unfold in a given sequence, which does not vary from child to child. Further, children cannot skip a stage of development, and they may get stuck at a particular stage for a number of reasons.

Recall from chapter three that the use of the word "development" can be confusing when we're discussing global awareness education. Development education has to do with specific social, economic, and political issues of survival and growth: food distribution, demographics, care for the environment, literacy, disarmament, and so on. Developmental theory has to do with the stages of a child's growth. Developmental theories are attractive to educators because they can be used to structure contents and methods of education that are relevant and accessible to children at given stages of growth. Determination of curriculum content is often based on developmental theory.

Here is a brief summary of one developmental scheme. It describes what basic knowledge and skills children can learn at given ages.

Infants and very young children use their senses to explore both their own bodies and concrete objects. They mouth, grasp, hit, and bang objects and gradually learn to manipulate them.

Preschool children learn names, numbers, colors, and how to categorize objects. They enjoy playing with language — especially the word "why." They also develop movement skills like running, jumping, hopping, and skipping.

Young school children continue to develop these skills and incorporate them in group activities. They enjoy riddles and jokes. Their fine motor skills increase, so that they can write, draw, and build models with some competence.

Older children in the primary grades can play games with rules. They become competitive. They enjoy telling stories.

Intermediate level children are good at learning and remembering facts. They can begin to understand how systems work, and thus are able to understand such concepts as interdependence.

Junior high students can begin to think abstractly. They like to argue the logic of a given point. They are concerned with what is "fair." They are also interested in the lifestyles of "heroes" (usually rock stars in our culture). They are fascinated with what is "far out" and unexpected.

High school students develop the capacity to analyze data and theories and to make abstract judgments. They can be quite idealistic at this age and extremely critical of hypocrisy.

There is, of course, much more to the cognitive abilities of children than this brief description suggests. The point is that developmental theory suggests that children have the capacity to learn certain data and skills at given stages in their development.

Application of this concept shapes the learning opportunities that are made available to children at different stages of their growth. For example, we don't try to teach algebra to seven-year-olds because they haven't yet developed the capacity to use logic in the way that doing algebra requires. According to the theory, the capacity is there. It's just not ready to be developed because the child has to develop other capacities first. The child needs to be exposed sequentially to information and experiences appropriate for his or her stage of development.

Social Development

Just as some theorists have proposed stages of cognitive development, others have proposed stages of psychosocial development. Probably the best-known of these theories is the so-called stages of man sequence described by Erik Erikson in his book *Childhood and Society*.[2] According to Erikson, human beings develop in stages according to a certain sequence of developmental issues. The first stage in his scheme is that of the infant, for whom the major issue is the development of trust. The psychosocial growth of the child depends on the infant's ability to learn to trust his or her environment. The stages then proceed through the development of autonomy and initiative in the preschool and early school years, industry in the middle school years, and identity in the teen years. (There are other stages for adulthood.) At each stage, Erikson also describes a less desirable outcome of development, such as mistrust instead of trust and isolation instead of identity.

Stages of Moral Development

Erikson ventures into the realm of moral development in his description of the development of virtues that correspond to the stages outlined above: hope, will, purpose, competence, and fidelity.[3] The best-known name in the field of moral development theory, however, is Lawrence Kohlberg.

Kohlberg proposed a series of stages in which the individual moves from a morality based on self-focused concerns through one based on social concerns to one based on concern for universal principles.[4] According to his theory, very young children "behave" because they fear punishment. At the next stage of development, children choose the "right" action because it gives them a feeling of satisfaction of their needs. The focus here is still on their own gratification. By the time a child reaches school age, he or she chooses to do right out of a desire to please those in authority (the "good boy/nice girl" orientation). Upholding the honor of the family or some other group with which one identifies is the fourth stage of development. This is the "law and order" stage. The emphasis in these two stages is on the social context of the individual: what others think. The fifth and sixth stages of making moral choices occur in a universal context. The individual considers the good of the community and, finally, the application of universal principles, such as justice, as the basis for moral decisions.

After developing his theory, Kohlberg expressed some ambivalence about the existence of the final stage. He also described a half stage between the fourth and the fifth stages, which corresponds roughly to adolescence in Erikson's scheme.[5] This stage is characterized by a disconcerting awareness of competing value systems, not all of them based on "moral" considerations. The individual becomes uncomfortable with the lack of a moral anchor and, ideally, moves on to the next stage. (Some educators would point out that many adults get stuck at stage four or at this stage, which does not necessarily correspond to the teen years.)

Criticisms of Developmental Theory

For Kohlberg, morality is reasoning about conflicting claims. Moral development occurs as individuals face crises. Erikson's theories also imply conflicting claims on the individual's psychosocial process. While human development is certainly a matter of evaluating alternatives and making choices, it may not be so dramatic and problematic as the language of these two theorists suggests. It could be that broader social and moral awareness develops as global awareness increases. Choices are then a response to an expanded point of view rather than to a crisis.

There is always a danger in setting up schemes for anything if parents or teachers take them as inflexible guidelines for growth. Both Erikson and Kohlberg try to incorporate many possibilities for development. They also avoid suggesting that they have cut the pattern for the perfect human being. Still, theories such as they have proposed cannot help but create expectations of certain kinds of behavior at various stages of a child's growth. ("According to Kohlberg, my child should be moving into the law and order stage, but he seems to be stuck in the good boy stage.") Parents and teachers will want to avoid this kind of determinism.

Psychologist Carol Gilligan has raised a more telling criticism of the work of Kohlberg, who was her colleague at Harvard. In her work entitled *In a Different Voice*, she points out the limitations of Kohlberg's research because he studied only the moral development of adolescent males.[6] Gilligan found that males tend to make moral decisions based on a hierarchy of values. Women tend to make moral decisions based on concern for relationships. Men subscribe to an ethic of justice, which Kohlberg defines as equality. Women subscribe to an ethic of care. In Kohlberg's scheme of things, women would be seen as stuck at the stage of concern for what others think. Gilligan proposes that the highest moral development depends on the interdependence of both an ethic of justice and an ethic of care.

Making Some Sense of Educational Theories

Theories are just that. They are efforts to organize information gained in various ways into a systematic explanation of some phenomenon. Theories can help us to think about and understand things, but they are not facts.

Theories about how children learn are useful when they help us to understand children's aptitudes, interests, social needs, and capacities for moral reasoning. They are not useful when they are used as yardsticks against which children are measured and then graded or labeled.

With that caveat in mind, let me offer my own completely unscientific theories about how children learn. These are based to some extent on what I have read and to a large extent on what I have experienced as a parent and educator.

1. The minds of children are marvelous, complex, and absorbent. Much of what human beings believe about life and the world around them is influenced in a lasting way by what they learn before they reach first grade.

2. Children are not miniature adults. Many parents don't know this. There are some behaviors that are perfectly appropriate for children at a particular age, such as throwing tantrums, saying "no" (the particular expertise of two-year-olds), and asking "why." Rebellion is an appropriate developmental behavior for teenagers.

In other words, there is such a thing as development in children's cognitive, social, and moral growth.

3. Everyone, including adults, learns best by experience.

4. Children learn more by self-initiated observation and imitation than they do by having information funneled into them.

5. The role of educators, both parents and teachers, is to provide children with a wide variety of experiences for observation and imitation, give them a vocabulary to talk about what they are seeing and doing, and then get out of the way.

6. When a learning situation involves values, children will learn more from the practice of parents and teachers than they will from pronouncements.

7. Children need to be able to make mistakes without fear of punishment. Making mistakes is part of the process of learning by experience. Making mistakes lets children know that they need to think of other ways to look at a problem or a situation. Telling a child what to do, or insisting that there is a "best" way of doing something, leads children to the conclusion that there is only one right way to do things. Parents and teachers can help children to remedy mistakes by suggesting alternative courses of action for consideration.

8. Children need to experience the consequences of their decisions and actions, except when that would result in psychic or physical injury. Parents and teachers do not do children a favor when they "rescue" them from the consequences of their choices. A child develops self-confidence, a sense of competence and a concern for the needs and feelings of others when he or she is able to "take charge" of a self-created situation.

9. Children don't need a lot of rules. They should help to develop the rules that they do need so that they understand why rules are necessary. This is also true for adults.

10. Adults should make a distinction between rules of social convention and rules of moral behavior. Hair length, curfews, dress codes, and traffic patterns in school hallways are all matters of social convention. Lying, cheating, stealing, and substance abuse are issues of moral behavior. Consequences for violating each type of rule should make clear the distinction between the two. In some homes and schools it's hard to tell the difference. In some homes and schools, hair length is a more serious issue than cheating.

11. Children live in the present moment. They can remember

past events, but they are not too skillful at making connections to the present. One of the tasks of education is to help children connect the past and the present in a way that promotes hope for the future.

This is particularly important for teenagers and young adults, who have not had enough life experience to realize that circumstances of a situation can change over time. Despair about the present can lead to hopelessness, particularly when a child has not had the opportunity to confront and cope successfully with obstacles. Adults who have confronted and mastered some of life's challenges can model hope, even when the present situation promotes pessimism. The capacity to hope is an important component of moral maturity and, by extension, of concern for others.

Implications for Global Awareness Education

Children are not born knowing all about the world or even knowing what they need to know about the world. Global awareness education is a lifelong process that builds on the developing capacities of human beings beginning in infancy.

Children need to learn to trust their own environment if they are to experience the world as a friendly place. Infants learn to trust when they receive consistent care and attention to their basic needs for care, affection, and security. A child who lacks these basic guarantees cannot trust the world at large — or the people in it.

Young children need to be exposed to a variety of learning experiences outside their immediate environment. They need to learn that "different" is interesting, not dangerous. They need to have their sense of awe and wonder fed by exposure to the beauties and adventures of the world around them.

Preschool and school-age children need to learn the basic rules of social interaction. They need to learn that rules are made for the sake of facilitating social interaction, and that rules can be changed when they no longer fit the situation for which they were made.

Respect for the needs, experiences, and values of others is crucial to developing global awareness. In a world characterized by pluralism, children need to be comfortable with looking at situations from a number of viewpoints. They need the security of their own value system at the same time that they recognize that it may be one among many.

Children who learn to take responsibility for their own actions will grow up to feel some responsibility for the fate of others. They will understand the concept of interdependence and realize that their actions affect the lives of others.

Lack of knowledge and understanding of global issues on the part of parents and teachers does not need to be an impediment to creating global awareness in children. Children will learn what's important from observing what their parents and teachers take an interest in. While children up to the age of nine or so tend to think that adults know everything, older children know better and actively resent "know-it-all" attitudes. Adults don't need to know the answers to everything. They do need to know how to teach children to find answers.

According to theories of moral development, real global awareness probably doesn't develop until middle age, when people have acquired enough information, life experience, and moral growth to focus objectively on the world beyond their immediate horizons. That perspective, however, is the sum of learning experiences that begin with the trust of the small child. In the preschool and primary grades, formation of positive attitudes toward the needs of others and assimilation of factual information continue the process. As the capacity for critical analysis and problem-solving develops, young people can learn to evaluate global realities and to recognize unjust global structures. With moral maturity comes the acceptance of responsibility for contributing to building a just global community.

You are probably thinking that all this theory sounds, well, too theoretical. How do you go about teaching the necessary information and awareness? The practical applications of these theories are the subject of the next chapter.

Summary

No one knows for certain how children learn, but there are a number of theories about their cognitive, social, and moral growth. These theories can help us understand what children are capable of learning about global awareness at different ages.

Parents and teachers do not have to be experts on global affairs in order to teach children about global awareness. Global awareness education is a lifelong process. Children will learn that it is important if they observe that parents and teachers think it is important.

Young children need to learn that the world is a friendly place that can be trusted. Preschool and school-age children can learn to observe the world around them and can begin to learn basic facts about other countries and other people. Older children can learn how to analyze data about global realities and recognize unjust systems.

At every stage of development, children need to learn to care for the needs of others and to take responsibility for their own actions. They need to be able to recognize and name relationships.

The goal of global awareness education is to equip the learner to work for justice in the world.

Chapter 6

Methods of Teaching
Global Awareness

~

EVEN IF YOU HAVE NO IDEA WHERE BHUTAN IS, and even if the intricacies of educational theory still confuse you, you can create a climate in your home or classroom that facilitates skills and attitudes necessary for global awareness. Global awareness education is much more than a curriculum with a particular content. It is also a process by which children learn to relate to the world and to other people with self-confidence and with respect for other cultures, other beliefs, other ways of making decisions.

Children will think that global awareness is important if their parents and teachers think it's important. A home or classroom where maps are displayed, where newspapers and news magazines are readily available, and where the day's news is a regular topic of discussion all give children a message that what's going on in the world beyond their community is important.

This is true even when the child is too young to read or to understand the complexities of world events. One of my earliest images of my mother is of her reading the daily newspaper and sipping the strong Louisiana coffee that is part of her heritage. My sister and I knew not to bother her during this sacred time, but my brother would crawl to her feet and attempt to bat the newspaper out of her hands to get her attention. He soon learned to wait until she was finished.

Keeping up with the news was, and is, important to my parents. When we finally got a television set, one of the programs we watched regularly was the nightly news with John Cameron Swayze. I can still remember the sponsor of the program: Timex! To this day, I am a "news junkie," no doubt due to the early influence of my parents.

66

Children absorb snatches of world news every day from television, radio, glances at headlines, overheard adult conversations, and discussions at school. It's a good idea to invite them into periodic discussions about what they see and hear. By the time a child reaches high school, regular discussion and analysis of world events should be part of the learning curriculum, both at home and in the classroom.

Developing Global Awareness Close to Home

Your own family history may be an excellent resource for developing global awareness in your children. Children love to hear stories about the members of their families, especially the oddballs! (In my family, one of the curiosities from several generations back is a man named Rice Garland, about whom it is always said that "he left under a cloud." No one seems to be quite sure what the cloud was.)

If your ancestors can be traced to other countries, you have a ready resource for helping your children to recognize their own global connections. Thumbing through family photo albums or listening to taped oral histories from senior members of the family fascinates most children.

One of the easiest ways to develop global awareness in children is to expose them on a regular basis to other cultures in your community. If you live and shop in a neighborhood that is culturally mixed, your children will have a good understanding of the diversity of the world's peoples. If the church you attend has a culturally diverse congregation, your children will learn the additional lesson that all kinds of people can share common beliefs. If their schools enroll students of various racial and ethnic origins and students who are differently abled, their learning environment itself will be a lesson in global awareness. If their sports teams, Scout troops, and other membership organizations are multicultural, they will learn to feel comfortable with children of races and ethnic origins other than their own. Such daily opportunities for contact also provide many informal opportunities for discussing differences, clearing up any misconceptions about them, and questioning stereotypes.

If you have a choice of ethnic restaurants in your community, you could make a habit of visiting them when the family dines out instead of the hamburger-and-styrofoam emporiums.

Instead of shopping for food exclusively in the local outlets of supermarket chains, try shopping in stores that carry ethnic foods. Take your children with you and let them choose a food that interests them. (On a recent trip to Toronto, I encountered a group of ten-year-olds on a field trip who had been turned loose with checklists in the city's extensive and interesting Asian market section. I'm not certain that I'd want to be the teacher responsible for their wanderings, but I'm sure they learned a lot about Asian cuisine!)

If there are no such opportunities for your children in your community, perhaps you should wonder why.

Public Life and Global Awareness

"Public life," says sociologist Parker Palmer, "is — simply and centrally — our life among strangers, strangers with whom our lot is cast, with whom we are interdependent whether we like it or not."[1] Public life is not just political life, which is the way many of us understand it. It is, rather, the life we share with other people whose names we do not know. When we become comfortable with public life, we learn the truth that "our identity is not to be found in our differences from others — in our superiorities and inferiorities — but in our common humanity."[2]

In the United States, many parents shelter their children from what Palmer calls "the company of strangers." Children are taught to be afraid of strangers, often for good reasons. But in some other cultures, strangers are treated as guests.

As a people, we tend to be fiercely individualistic. We are possessive about "our" property. We spend much of our time, energy, and money furnishing, decorating, and maintaining the spaces in which we live. When we join civic associations, it is usually for the sake of protecting our property and our rights. We are concerned about the safety of our neighborhoods and about the threat to our property values when "outsiders" move in. Instead of thinking "the world is coming to our door," we are more apt to think "there goes the neighborhood." Our children pick up these messages, spoken and unspoken, about our priorities and our privatism.

Children need experiences of public life if they are to feel comfortable in a society where the world is coming to their doorsteps. By public life, I mean the opportunity to mix with strangers in everyday settings without necessarily having to interact with them.

For example, a child riding the subway to work with me in the morning would see people of various racial and ethnic backgrounds and would hear several languages being spoken. He or she would also see a young man maneuvering his way into and out of the subway car in a motorized wheel chair, a blind man whose seeing eye dog occasionally bumps into me on the escalator in the subway station, and some hearing-impaired students who manage to sign to one another even as they try not to lose their balance when the train lurches to a stop. When these sights and sounds become part of the stuff of everyday life, and when they can be noted and discussed comfortably, children cease to regard people who are different as strange or threatening.

How many children — and parents — use public transportation on a regular basis? If your community is anything like mine, not many.

Parades, political rallies, civic celebrations, ethnic festivals, church bazaars, and sports events are occasions for people from varied backgrounds to mix with one another on common ground and become more aware of one another in a casual way. Parks, community playgrounds, sidewalk cafes, museums, and galleries are public spaces where people can enjoy themselves among strangers. Providing children opportunities to experience these public events and spaces increases their appreciation of the diversity of human life.

Another way to get children involved in public life is to introduce them to participation in private voluntary organizations (PVOs): church and community groups that feed the poor, environmental action groups, advocacy groups, and other groups where people with common interests can come together. Parents should not force their own group affiliations on their children, but should allow children to choose groups that suit their own interests, since many PVOs are geared primarily to adult involvement. For example, parents may choose to join Bread for the World and participate in advocacy for hunger relief legislation. Children who share their parents' concern for the hungry will probably prefer a "hands on" activity, like preparing food for the local soup kitchen, or membership in a children's organization, like the Holy Childhood Association, that helps hungry children.

Voluntary Organizations and Development Education

Besides providing opportunities for people with common interests and concerns to come together at the local level, national private voluntary organizations are excellent sources of materials for development education. Many of them deal with the problems of hunger, illiteracy, environmental degradation, discrimination, and other development issues. Your local library may have materials from some of these groups. The education department of your church can direct you to other PVOs, depending on your area of interest. You can also be on the lookout for news stories that mention organizations involved in your areas of interest.

"Service projects" are required of many children for school credit, religious programs, service club membership, or Scouting achievements. Children who choose to deal with a global problem (hunger, illiteracy, racial discrimination, polluted water, waste disposal, among others) on a local level benefit not only from the experience of volunteering but also from acquiring a local perspective of a global problem. Real awareness of global problems begins with the lived experience of the problem close to home.

Learning from Play

Young children begin to acquire global awareness skills through play. Play is the work that children do. It is the "job" of young children, a job that is crucial for their social development.

Up to the age of three or so, children don't really play together. They exhibit what educators call "parallel play," play that goes on at the same time and in the same space as the play of other children without any real interaction between them most of the time. This is not to say that young children don't care about each other. Even a young child may try to soothe the distress of another child by offering the use of a favorite "comfort" item, like a bottle or a security blanket.

Through play, children become comfortable with the world around them. Play is a child's way of ordering his or her environment. Play teaches children the relationship between cause and effect. It also helps them to begin to take responsibility for their behavior. Play allows children to feel competent.[3]

Structured, adult-directed activities are not play. Authentic play is initiated and structured by the child. Play provides the intrinsic motivation that children need to learn. According to early childhood educators, "play may be the most important process through which children learn to adapt to the world and become more mature."[4]

Children do not need a lot of toys in order to play creatively. What they do need are varieties of materials from which to construct their own toys. In a preschool setting, there should be enough play materials available so that children will not need to squabble over who gets to use what. Many incidents of aggressive behavior in preschool classrooms originate because of insufficient play materials.

Children in Third World countries are adept at constructing playthings out of simple materials such as buttons, string, wire, bottles, small stones, scraps of cloth, and empty boxes. "Manufactured" toys are unknown in many parts of the world; children make their own.

A missionary in Tanzania describes the ingenuity of the children with whom she works like this:

> Take some old rags ... bind them together with strips of sisal, and what do we have?? A FOOTBALL, of course!! In the evening when the sun is not so hot, you can find groups of boys all ages and sizes playing football (barefooted) and thoroughly enjoying themselves.
>
> Old boxes and tins are much too precious to throw away. Any cardboard box can be transformed into a truck or land-rover, and the tins make good wheels. All this is done by hand with the help of some sharp stones. One of our local plants has a very sticky sap and makes great glue for sticking the car together. The boys can spend hours assembling and making their "gari" — the outcome is really amazing!
>
> The girls often make dolls from clay and carry them on their backs. When the wild flowers are in blossom, the girls make necklaces and bracelets with the flowers.[5]

Children in the United States can also learn to enjoy toys they have made themselves. Most parents have had the experience of watching a child play for hours with the box a new toy came in while the toy itself is ignored.

While adults should not attempt to structure the young child's play, parents and teachers can provide an environment for play that introduces global themes. For example, dolls can represent various ethnic backgrounds. Children can learn songs and games from other countries. Story books can feature the everyday experiences of children of different cultures. "Different" does not necessarily mean "foreign." Middle-class children will benefit from stories about inner-city children in the United States, like those by John Steptoe.[6] Older children will enjoy stories about heroes and historical figures from other countries.

Storytelling — Expanding the Child's Viewpoint

Storytelling, while not strictly play if it is initiated by adults, is an important learning experience for children. Children enjoy telling stories of their own composition, and adults can learn what children are thinking by listening carefully and respectfully to these stories. Using dolls to tell a story or to enact a troublesome situation, such as hurt feelings over a racist or sexist remark, helps children to imagine the feelings of others, an important step in developing global awareness.

Storytelling is an art. Good storytellers are a community treasure and should be invited often into the elementary classroom. Your library may be a good source for information about a local storytellers' guild in your area.

When storytellers represent the traditions of other cultures, children get a first-hand impression of the riches that other cultures have brought to the United States. Alice McGill, a professional storyteller based in Columbia, Maryland, travels across the country teaching children the African-American tradition of "call-and-response," a session that brings lessons on slavery and the Civil War to life. Storytelling, she says, inspires self-confidence in children and helps teachers "to get across that last entrance skill or the times tables."[7]

Games — Expanding the Child's Social Perspective

In order for a game to be played, children must make the rules or, at least, agree to the rules that go with the game. Even if the rules don't make sense, or if they "won't work," adults should refrain from imposing structure on games children play, including board games. So long as the participants in the game agree to the rules they establish, anything goes. Children will find out quickly enough if the rules they make impede the progress of the game.

Learning to make rules and then to revise them when they don't work is an important element in developing problem-solving and negotiation skills.

During the preschool years, children play games for the sake of the pleasure of the activity and not for the sake of winning. Around the age of seven, they become more interested in games with rules — and with winning. The element of competition enters into play activities.

Competition Can Be Constructive

Some educators discourage competition in games and in other learning situations because they believe that it impedes the development of cooperative behavior. Since promoting cooperative attitudes is one of the goals of global awareness education, competition as a form of social interaction may appear to be negative. While cooperative behavior is an important social skill, children also develop an awareness of others by competing with them.

Once children begin to play games to win, they need to develop strategies for winning. They need to try to think the way the other players are thinking in order to "second guess" their opponents. Developing a competitive attitude is one indication that a child is beginning to think in terms of what others may be thinking. The desire to compete can also lead to awareness of the need to negotiate so that rules are "fair."

Developing a competitive spirit is part of a child's social development. Competition can be healthy when it leads the child to consider the perspective of others. Competition becomes harmful when winning becomes all important, or when competitive games leave some children feeling isolated or incompetent. Games that involve an element of luck provide a good balance to games that require particular skills or abilities. Parents and teachers should introduce children to games of both kinds.[8]

Cooperative board games are a good way of teaching social skills, especially when the games can involve the whole family. Several games of this type are based on scenarios that teach global awareness.[9] Games that involve competition between teams combine elements of both cooperation and competition.

Competition in the classroom may be inevitable, at least among elementary-level children, since competition is a natural part of children's development. (Among older children, competition for good grades may be discouraged by peer pressure if academic achievement is not valued.) Competitive games contribute to children's development, but motivating children to learn through competition gives them the wrong incentive for learning.

Children do not need to compete in the classroom so much as they need to have their academic efforts recognized and commended. A child who appears to place too much emphasis on being "the best" academically may need attention more than he or she needs A's. Cooperative learning, especially working in groups, teaches children that many heads working together can usually come up with better ideas, information, and solutions to dilemmas than can several heads working against one another.

Global educator Jean Houston likes to tell the story of what can happen when people learn to solve problems cooperatively. She points to one tribe in Africa that solves a problem by singing and drumming the problem. The members of the tribe dance the problem. Then they dream it. Then they talk about it, and dance while they're talking. Then they solve the problem. (In many African tribes, solving problems by consensus is traditional.) This particular tribe has no neuroses and no war, and there are women among its elders.[10]

What would happen if you tried this method of problem-solving the next time a family disagreement erupts?

Parker Palmer has described another method of cooperative problem-solving based on a Quaker practice called "the clearness committee." The process begins when a couple writes out the problem along with some background information. They then invite five or six others to read what they have written and discuss it with them. There is only one rule: the "committee" members may only ask questions. They may not suggest solutions. The couple must answer all questions in the presence of the group. As the questions go deeper, the couple finds answers.[11]

What would happen if you tried this method of problem-solving the next time a fight breaks out during recess?

Strategies for Cooperation

Being able to understand the feelings of others is a necessary skill for problem-solving and, especially, for conflict resolution. Children who develop problem-solving and conflict resolution skills early will help to shape a world where all sides of a problem can be considered without resorting to war.

As with other global awareness skills, learning takes time, and development of skills depends on a child's emotional maturity. Still, it's never too early to start.

Quarrels engendered by sibling rivalry provide many opportunities for introducing and practicing conflict resolution skills. Parents and caregivers who remain calm, refuse to take sides, and insist that each child consider the other child's feelings are setting the stage for conflict resolution and a cooperative atmosphere.

Here are some basic rules for settling disputes that apply equally well in the home and in the classroom:[12]

1. Determine what the dispute or disagreement is about. Give each side a chance to state the case without interruption. Teach children to use "I" statements to describe their own perceptions and feelings, not "you" statements that accuse the other of causing a reaction.

2. Have each side state the other side's position. (This will probably provoke further dispute, but keep at it until there's consensus. In some cases, the dispute might end right here if the parties recognize a misunderstanding.)

3. Ask each side to propose one or more solutions, and then predict the other side's probable response to each proposal. This means stepping into the other person's shoes to imagine how the proposal would affect him or her.

4. Consider together the consequences of each proposal. Play "what is the worst/best thing that will happen if we choose this alternative?" The purpose of this step is to have children consider cause and effect: "If I do this, then that will happen."

5. Let children choose a proposal they can both agree on that meets everyone's needs. Once the plan is carried out, evaluate its effectiveness. If the proposed solution doesn't work, try one of the other proposals. When children have had some experience making choices, they can be encouraged to negotiate the solution they prefer with the understanding that they are responsible for the consequences of their choices.

If adults co-opt this process by directing or limiting choices, then the child learns nothing. While the process is time consuming at first, it is worth the effort. "A child who can think of five ways to get something is more likely to get it in a constructive way than a child who can think of only one way," according to parent educator Elizabeth Crary.[13] Children also learn from this process two other lessons that are critical to developing global awareness: (1) people can solve their own problems; and (2) people have the right to be involved in making decisions that affect their lives.

The goal of teaching conflict resolution skills is the development of cooperative attitudes. When children realize they can work together to find solutions that satisfy everyone, the occasions for conflict decrease. They also become more interested in cooperating than in competing when they realize that they can get their needs met more dependably through cooperation than through competition.

Another missionary in Tanzania discovered this truth when she organized a foot race among her students. She was surprised when the fastest runners slowed down to wait for the others. "It's more fun to cross the finish line together," they explained.[14] When children learn to cooperate, everyone wins.

Providing Experiences That Build Global Awareness

Children who have had many diverse experiences will have a large reservoir of ideas upon which they can draw when they need ideas for problem-solving. As much as possible children should be exposed to the "workings" of their community through trips to airports, dairies, farms, police and fire stations, hospitals, newspaper plants, courthouses, wholesale markets, and other places of business. Vacation trips to unfamiliar parts of the country also provide the scripts for learning about diverse ways people live and work. Young children will enjoy imitating what they see on such outings. Older children will add their impressions to their repertoire of information about what the world beyond their doorstep is like. Such experiences introduce students to the concept of interdependent systems.

Becoming aware of how systems work is crucial to an understanding of the global concept of interdependence. Beginning at or about the age of nine, children can be taught to look for interrelationships in systems.

One of the effective ways to teach the interdependence of systems is to have children trace the origins and delivery of goods with which they are familiar: the building materials contained in their homes, for example, or the foods they eat for breakfast. One popular exercise in the "ingredients of interdependence" traces the production of a candy bar.[15] The ingredients gathered from around the world, the fuel and trucks used to transport them, the copper used for the boilers at the chocolate factory, and the paper used to wrap the candy bar are all part of a chain that involves many countries, affects employment and the balance of trade, and raises questions about diet and health for the consumer. By tracing the manufacturing process, children learn the concept of the interdependence of many systems.

Understanding interdependence teaches children to look for connections and patterns, to recognize gaps or inconsistencies in information, and to appreciate the complexities of most issues. Children will learn to withhold hasty judgments of other cultures when they realize that people can be trapped by economic or political or social systems. They will gradually become aware that unjust systems are made up of individual actions that contribute to a corporate effect. In other words, unjust systems are built on individual actions.

We have a tendency to teach children to label things quickly and to look for instant solutions to problems. (These characteristics are typical of ESTJ types!) Most children don't like ambiguity, and we don't do a very good job of teaching them to live with it. (I can still recall the grumbling of a tenth-grader who walked out of one of my classes mumbling, "Questions, questions is all we ever get in here — never any answers!") Helping children to be comfortable with ambiguity is one way of teaching them not to jump to conclusions about other cultures and other people.

Infusing Information

Shaping attitudes and teaching cooperative skills is not all there is to global awareness education. Children need to learn facts about other peoples, countries and cultures. This information is not innate; it must be learned. The question is how.

Recall our previous discussion about play. It is the most effective way that children learn because it is initiated and structured by the child. Teaching information of any kind is more effective when the process of learning is chosen and structured by the child. How can this be done in a classroom setting with a prescribed curriculum?

Take a look around your classroom or your child's classroom.

What does the setting of the classroom say about the teaching methods? Are students' desks arranged in groups where they can learn from one another — or are all the desks lined up facing the teacher's desk? What do the bulletin boards, posters, and other learning aids in the classroom say about learning priorities? Global awareness education in the classroom begins with the classroom setting.

Do students have the opportunity to work in groups and to share ideas and efforts? Are children grouped in such a way that their personalities and skills complement one another — or are they grouped only by ability, which encourages competition for grades? Instead of separating "gifted and talented" students from their classmates, why not make them "peer teachers" by distributing them among classroom groups?

Do children have a say in rules that affect their participation in classroom activities — or does the teacher make all the rules? Are children offered choices of ways of doing an assignment so that their skills and preferred styles of learning can be engaged — or do assignments always follow a predictable and inflexible format? How learning activities are structured is itself a lesson in developing attitudes that contribute to global awareness.

Lectures by the teacher are the least effective method of teaching information about global awareness because they put the student in a passive mode. Activities such as role playing scenarios involve students and help them to stand in the shoes of other people. Case study approaches also personalize learning when, for example, students are asked to imagine what their lives would be like if they were a girl in a Muslim society or a teenager in a refugee camp.

Educators agree that simulation games are effective teaching tools at every level. Once older students become accustomed to this style of learning, they can form working groups to research and construct simulations for a variety of experiences. Constructing a simulation requires that students understand both the facts and the feelings of the situation being studied, such as the problems of hunger, homelessness, or environmental degradation. Simulation games should always include careful preparation and follow-up. Students should have enough information about the simulated situation to be able to "act" responsibly. A thorough debriefing should follow the end of the game: What happened? How did it feel? How is the game like reality? What issues were raised? What actions can or should be taken?

Occasional multicultural experiences or spontaneous "mini-lessons" are perceived as nothing more than diversions from the "real" curriculum. In order for global awareness education to be effective, it must permeate the curriculum. Robert Muller, who has been both Assistant Secretary General of the United Nations and chancellor of the United Nations University of Peace in Costa Rica, has developed a "world core curriculum" that emphasizes "everything that has to do with the planet and everything that has to do with human rights." The curriculum is being implemented at the Robert Muller School in Arlington, Texas.[16]

Teachers can examine their own prescribed courses of study with an eye to making changes in content and concept that will emphasize global awareness. One of the most effective ways of doing this is through the infusion method. This method does not so much require a change in the content of what is taught as it suggests a way of permeating content with global awareness. Since most teachers are required to teach an established curriculum, this is a practical and interesting approach to teaching a global perspective.

The infusion method may be used to teach both concepts and information. Concepts are best taught by modeling them. We have already discussed such global awareness concepts as interdependence, cooperation, justice, and human rights. Beyond discussing them with children, we can teach children by our example how to incorporate awareness of them into our lifestyles.

Infusing information that develops global awareness requires some planning at first, but it can create interest in what might otherwise be a dull lesson. Infusion throughout the curriculum can be a challenge shared by all the members of a teaching team.

Infusion makes learning fun. It introduces the unexpected into a routine activity. It makes connections between the various parts of the school curriculum.

Infusing global awareness into a curriculum means that learning activities are permeated with information about other parts of the world. For example, math word problems use situations from another culture: "A woman in rural Africa spends one hour per day collecting firewood, one hour collecting water, one and a half hours pounding and grinding corn, and one hour cooking. What percentage of her day does the woman spend in preparing food?"

Sooner of later, someone is going to ask, "Why does she have to collect firewood?" or "Why doesn't she just turn on the faucet?" Learning that began in a math lesson then spills over into the social studies curriculum and leads to discussion of the effects of poverty.

Global awareness can be infused into every area of the curriculum. Besides learning to spell words, children can also learn the languages from which they originated. Reading and writing assignments can focus on life situations in other cultures. A social studies lesson about neighborhood or community interdependence can include comparison and contrast with neighborhood and community life in another country. Science activities can center around global implications of the topic under study, especially in relation to development issues.

Parents can get into the act by taking a close look at their children's learning materials and suggesting ways that global themes can be incorporated into the curriculum. Children can also suggest global perspectives once they understand the infusion method. They may enjoy making up their own math problems or suggesting ways to include a global perspective in classroom projects.

The PTA can join the effort by taking a broad view of the school's curriculum and environment and suggesting ways to incorporate a global perspective. How about painting a map of the world in the entry space, on the auditorium floor, or on the playground? Why not work with the librarian to assess the quality and quantity of global awareness materials in the resource center? Perhaps PTA funds could be used to purchase subscriptions for the teachers' lounge to the *Washington Post*, the *New York Times*, the *Christian Science Monitor*, or some other newspaper or news magazine that covers international news in detail.

The possibilities for using the infusion method are endless and limited only by the creativity — and time — of the teaching team. Infusion takes planning, perspective, and perseverance. Throwing in a fact here or an infused lesson there doesn't involve children in the learning process and may result in a distorted perspective. To be effective, infusion must be consistent. When it is consistent, it creates a climate of global awareness.

The United Nations and Global Awareness
No discussion of resources for global awareness education would be complete without mention of the United Nations. At present,

it is the only forum for international discussion of concerns that affect all humanity. Its history has been marked by disagreement over its goals, organization, leadership, and, especially, its funding, but it remains a viable source of hope for promoting the welfare of the planet and all its people.

The United Nations is a good source of information about global topics. High school students can also be introduced to the Model UN program, which helps to globalize the curriculum and teach conflict resolution skills. Children may be interested in learning about the activities of UNICEF, the United Nations Children's Fund.[17]

Getting Started

Teaching children about global awareness begins with the awareness of parents and teachers. We can't teach what we don't know, but any teacher can tell you that one of the best ways to learn something is to have to teach it. One of the most exciting aspects of preparing lessons with a global awareness perspective is realizing that there is so much information available once you begin looking for it. The next two chapters offer some of that information.

No matter what subject you teach, infusing global awareness can make teaching more interesting for you. There's a world of possibilities waiting for you!

Summary

Children learn the importance of global awareness from the example and interest of their parents and teachers. There are many resources for teaching global awareness: family history, diverse cultures in the community and in public life, private voluntary organizations, newspapers, books, magazines, and other publications.

Young children begin to acquire global awareness skills through play. Play is the work of children and is crucial for their social development. Toys and games can teach not only cooperative skills, but also information that helps to develop global awareness. Competition in games is a normal part of the social development of children and is healthy when it leads the child to consider the perspectives of others.

Cooperative learning methods contribute to global awareness, as does the practice of conflict resolution skills. When children master these skills, they also learn that people can solve their own problems and that people have the right to be involved in making decisions that affect their lives.

Providing children with experiences that expose them to the world beyond their doorstep helps them to understand the interdependence of human life. They will also become aware of the ways individual actions can contribute to the building of unjust systems.

One of the most effective ways of teaching global awareness is through the infusion method. Although it requires time and creativity on the part of the teacher, it is a practical and interesting way of developing global awareness in students.

Chapter 7

Teaching Awareness: The Environment

~

WHEN I WAS IN GRADUATE SCHOOL, a favorite hangout between classes was the "coffee lounge," a basement room equipped with a few tables and chairs and a coffeemaker. A student who had a work scholarship was responsible for keeping a steady supply of coffee and styrofoam cups available. One day, with gentle good will, two students sat down in front of the coffeemaker to protest the "slaughter of the styros." Only when the coffee drinkers promised to bring in mugs for future use were we allowed to consume our caffeine that day. We did — and the shelf full of mugs made a homey addition to what had been a rather barren environment. Because the only available water for washing the mugs was in the nearby men's room, the men also took on the housekeeping responsibilities!

It was fun then. The protest was light-hearted, and the remedy to the problem was painless.

Ten years later, I attended a conference of missionaries concerned about environmental problems. (In Third World countries, survival is linked to the fate of the environment. The natural world also inspires music, art, and religion — so care for the earth is part of missionary activities.) What I heard at that conference was that the degradation of our earth will be beyond remedy by the year 2000 if we don't change our lifestyles immediately. A report from the United Nations Environment Programme (UNEP) says the same thing:

> If we continue to abuse nature, by the end of this century ... a third of our planet's productive land will be so eroded it will be useless. With the ensuing loss of habitat, a million

species could be exterminated — the most terrible loss of life in history.[1]

In the early days of the feminist movement, women would talk about the moment when they experienced a "click" — a sudden awareness of what feminism was all about. Sometimes it happened on the heels of a blatantly sexist remark. Sometimes an experience of being excluded because of being a woman produced the "click."

For me, that missionary conference was an ecological "click." It was not fun, and the solutions to the problems presented will not be painless.

A New Curriculum: Reduce, Reuse, Recycle

It's time to teach a new three R's: reduce, reuse, recycle. All three come under the heading of the big R: responsibility for the care of our planet home. As the threat of nuclear war recedes, we can see a much greater threat to our survival looming: the destruction of our environment. Wangari Maathai, founder of the Kenyan Green Belt Movement and chair of the National Council of Women of Kenya, puts it this way:

> I am concerned about the wounds and bleeding sores on the naked body of the earth. Have we not seen the long-term effects of these bleeding sores? The famine? The poverty? The chemical and nuclear accidents? The small wars and deaths in so many parts of the world? When we have seen all these calamities, have we done no more than ask: Who is responsible? For me, personally, I know that I may be responsible for some of it. I am sure that everybody else is responsible for some of it. We are responsible directly or indirectly. We are all of us strangling the earth.[2]

In the Beginning...

For the Christian, care for creation is a moral imperative. The very first chapter of Genesis tells us that God's creation was *tov* — good — and that the crown of creation, humankind, was *mazel tov* — very good. A key passage in the Christian understanding of the relation between human beings and the rest of creation is Genesis 1:28, which reads "Be fruitful and multiply, and fill the earth and subdue it; and have dominion over the fish of the sea and over the birds of the air and over every living thing that moves upon the earth" (RSV).

As for the Present...

Over the past century or two, we've taken that passage rather literally. As several environmentalists have pointed out, "our abiding faith in technology all goes back to the mechanistic philosophies of Descartes and Newton, which viewed nature as raw material existing solely for human exploitation."[3] That viewpoint had some precedent in the literal interpretation of the words "subdue" and "have dominion." (Some translations use the word "conquer.") In the context of the difficult topography of the Middle East, where the Genesis story was first told, God's command made sense as a matter of survival.

But Genesis goes on. Sin enters the world, and the result is the Flood from which only a few are saved. According to the myth, God starts over. This time, God's covenant is made with all living things, not just human beings (Genesis 9:1–17). Human beings are one with all of creation. Humankind is entrusted with the care of the earth, as stewards of God's creation.

This viewpoint of the integrity of creation is developed in the Gaia idea, to which environmentalists often refer. In Greek mythology, Gaia was the mother goddess of the earth. The Gaia hypothesis, articulated in the 1960s by the British inventor and scientist James Lovelock, proposes that all the organisms of the earth act as one organism in regulating and maintaining its own environment. While this theory is regarded as merely controversial on the level of nonhuman life, it clearly meets some contradictions in the evidence of human activity.

In 1987, the World Commission on Environment and Development produced a widely-quoted report on the relationship between unsound economic activity and environmental degradation entitled *Our Common Future*. The chair of the commission, Norwegian Prime Minister Gro Harlem Brundtland, noted in the report that

> the Earth is one but the world is not. We all depend on one biosphere for sustaining our lives. Yet each community, each country, strives for survival and prosperity with little regard for its impact on others.[4]

The Christian churches have been slow to respond to the ecological crisis, but many of them are beginning to react. Pope John Paul II issued a document entitled *Peace with God the Creator, Peace with All of Creation* in observance of the World Day of Peace on January 1, 1990. In it, he accused First World nations of "unbridled consumption," which is a major contributor to environmental degradation. He also criticized Third World countries that "recklessly continue to damage the environment through industrial pollutants, radical deforestation or unlimited exploitation of non-renewable resources." The pope also said that First World nations should not expect Third World nations to adhere to ecological standards that industrialized nations ignore.[5]

Some environmentalists, especially those in the Third World, have gone further in suggesting that the industrialized nations should be held responsible for cleaning up global pollution, since they are the ones who have created most of it. Furthermore, Third World nations heavily saddled by development debt must first spend limited financial resources for immediate survival needs before they can be spent for remedial purposes. (Fair? Maybe not. Just? What do you think? What would your children or your students think? Do they clean up after themselves — or do you?)

Getting Back to the Basics

Children need to learn a basic law of ecology: everything is connected to everything else. The Native American culture teaches us this truth. In 1855, in a letter to President Franklin Pierce, Chief Seattle of the Duwamish tribe wrote: "Humankind has not woven the web of life. We are but one thread within it. Whatever we do to the web, we do to ourselves. All things are bound together. All things connect. Whatever befalls the Earth befalls also the children of the Earth."[6]

Children can learn to think in these terms if they are taught to consider systematically the consequences of their own actions.

Consider the following scenario. Wendy doesn't feel like walking to soccer practice, so she asks her big brother to drive her. He does — and he does some more driving while he's out, burning up a gallon of gas. Multiply Wendy and her obliging brother by the thousands of other needless excursions made every day that burn gasoline. (In the time that it takes you to read this sentence, more than forty thousand gallons of gasoline will be burned by drivers in the United States.[7]) Put the profits from the sale of that gasoline in the pockets of petroleum producers in some Middle Eastern countries.

For some of them, owning a dagger with an ivory hilt is a sign of prosperity. The market for ivory increases. Ivory hunters slaughter elephants in several African countries in order to harvest their ivory tusks.[8] In just ten years (from 1979 to 1989), the population of elephants is halved.

Elephants achieve their bulk by eating about three hundred pounds of vegetation daily. In doing so, their foraging creates open spaces and water holes for other animals. They are "architects of the environment."[9] Without them, the landscape is irrevocably changed, to the detriment of other forms of life.

All because the Wendys of the world didn't want to walk? Or is the slaughter of elephants in Africa someone else's fault?

Recognizing the Global Impact of Personal Action

"Think globally, act locally." It's not easy to teach children to think beyond their local environment, but it can be done. Young children do have a naive egocentricity that lets them think they are the cause of everything that happens in their immediate environment. Parents and teachers can build on this tendency to help children recognize situations in which their behavior does have an impact on the environment.

Most children, however, simply cannot imagine anything on a truly global scale. Children will think the elephant tusk scenario has nothing to do with them because it is far removed from their experience. Our task is to convince them that their actions, however insignificant they may seem, do have a "domino effect," especially when combined with the actions of other people.

Teaching children to think in terms of cause and effect is a good beginning. Small children may be able to think only in terms of one or two steps of the above scenario. ("Riding in the car when you don't need to wastes gas. Wasting gas isn't good for the earth. Wendy should walk if she can.") Intermediate level children can recognize the cause-and-effect sequence of the scenario. If you scramble the steps of the sequence, they can probably put them in proper order after some discussion. Older students should be able to construct the scenario if given the basic facts and a statement of the problem. ("Kids' unnecessary driving should be reduced because it is contributing to the destruction of wildlife in Africa.") They will also be able to recognize that the scenario is rather simplistic. ("There are other reasons for the degradation of the environment in Africa." "Unnecessary consumption of gasoline is also causing other problems, like air pollution, closer to home." "I read that the ban on ivory is causing problems in Zaire, where there are too many elephants, because people there count on the ivory trade to make a living.")

Act Locally, Think Globally

Dealing with global issues on a local level also helps students to expand their thinking. Children become aware of environmental problems in a number of ways. The most effective education builds on children's personal experiences of concern for the environment. They don't learn much from being talked at. They do learn from the example of parents and teachers. In homes and schools where recycling and conservation are practiced, children will inevitably ask "why." Care for the environment requires conscious and consistent effort, which children will initially resist if it's not convenient — and it usually isn't.

When it comes to teaching environmental concern, parents and teachers need to practice what they preach. As one parent notes, "To do any less is to convey to our children that planet-protection practices are optional. In the world we've known, they have been. In the world our children inherit, they can't be."[10]

One of the best ways to teach concern for the environment is to get children outdoors. Young children enjoy discovering the wonders of nature, and "nature walks" are a popular staple of the preschool curriculum. As they walk and explore, have children note the kinds of trash they find. Help them to figure out what kinds of trash decompose and what kinds don't. ("Why does a dead leaf disappear? Why doesn't a fast food container disappear? Which one can be recycled?") They'll learn a basic lesson about the meaning of "biodegradable" and the difference between "organic" and "inorganic" substances.

Older children can also make their own environmental excursions. As they walk, they can pick up trash. If much of it is from a recognizable source, such as fast food containers, they can write to the business concerned and suggest solutions to the disposal problem. (Let them brainstorm some ideas!) Younger children can also pick up trash and then dictate a letter to parents, teachers, or older siblings to be sent to the source responsible for producing the trash.

Through "hands-on" activities, children can recognize the cause-and-effect scenarios that harm the environment. Parents and teachers also increase children's awareness of environmental problems by exposing them to the beauties of the world around them — seashore, mountains, deserts, forests — and the infinite varieties of natural life. Children who learn the names of the flowers, animals, birds, trees, and insects they meet will acquire a respect for the uniqueness of living things. Young children, especially, are curious about the world around them and enjoy being able to name plants and pets and birds and bugs.

Parents and teachers can also be alert to timely opportunities for introducing children to environmental issues. Field trips to places that show evidence of environmental degradation are instructive, especially when they are followed by research about the problem and advocacy for change. A bad case of sunburn can lead to a discussion of the destruction of the ozone layer. An asthma attack, a local "air hazard" alert, or a smoggy day open up the possibility of learning something about the causes of air pollution. Building on a child's immediate awareness or experience is the best possible way to introduce environmental issues.

When we discuss environmental issues, it's important to keep in mind the goal of our teaching: to have children understand the need for sustainable development. This means that we want them to learn to use the earth's resources in such a way that the resources meet our needs and are renewed and available for future generations. We want them to learn the big R: responsibility for the earth's resources. We do this by teaching them the three R's: reduce, reuse, recycle.

The basic method for teaching environmental awareness begins with the child's experience. From that teachable moment, the lesson plan, formal or informal, looks something like this:

1. Ask children to state their assumptions about what was observed or experienced. Why is the park littered with trash? What kind of trash is it? Who left it there? Where did it come from?

2. Have children gather evidence and information about the problem. Why doesn't some of the trash decompose? Who is

supposed to clean it up? What is the best way to get rid of it? Asking someone who knows something about the problem is one way to get answers. For example, sanitation workers and groundskeepers may have some ideas about the sources of trash. Officials of the local government should have information about what's being done to address the problem. Magazines and newspapers are full of information about the problem of waste disposal and proposals for solving it. (Disposing of them is part of the problem!) Taking a field trip to a waste disposal or recycling facility can provide a useful perspective on the scope of the issue.

3. Check assumptions against the gathered evidence and information. What new understandings have developed?

4. Ask children to propose some solutions. Brainstorming or strategizing in groups is usually more effective than trying to figure things out alone. Consider any proposal, no matter how far-fetched it sounds at first.

5. Have children decide on personal actions that can be taken to solve the problem. ("I can reduce my use of wrappings and packagings. I can reuse shopping bags, disposable cups, and plastic food containers. I can recycle cans and bottles.")

6. Encourage children to advocate changes. Boycott companies whose products are contributing to the problem, and let them know why. If the people who made the mess can be identified, let them know about the problem and proposed solutions.

7. Show children how to tell other people what they have learned and what they are doing about it. Write letters to local newspapers. If a whole class of students is studying the problem, sign everyone's name. Make a video demonstrating the learning project, and show it to other classes. Put on a waste disposal awareness program for the next PTA meeting.

8. Let children know how to network with other organizations — local, national, or international — that share their concerns. Sharing resources and information divides the effort and multiplies the effect! It also helps to globalize the issue.

Now let's consider three global problems that might begin to be solved by local awareness and action. You can then use the above method of building awareness, action, and advocacy to talk about specific solutions.

The Problem of Polluted Air

Unless you live in an area that is removed from industry and transportation routes, you shouldn't have too much trouble helping children to become aware of the problem of air pollution. Getting stuck in traffic on a warm day (with the automobile's windows down) creates instant awareness. So does living downwind of an industrial area that produces pollutants. The Environmental Protection Agency (EPA) estimates that four out of ten people in the United States live in areas where the air is often unhealthy to breathe.[11]

Air pollution does more than just cause health problems. On a global scale, three major environmental problems have to do with air quality: acid rain, the greenhouse effect, and destruction of the ozone layer.

Acid rain is caused by the burning of fossil fuels, particularly coal and oil. The nitrogen and sulfur oxides given off primarily by power plants and also by gasoline engines are absorbed into the atmosphere and then fall as acid rain, destroying forests, polluting bodies of water, and killing aquatic life. Acid rain has destroyed forests in the northeastern part of the United States as well as 50 percent of the forests in Germany.[12] In Canada, fourteen thousand lakes have been polluted by acid rain, more than half of which comes from air pollution in the United States. Norway and Sweden are the reluctant recipients of acid rain that is precipitated by pollutants that originate in the United Kingdom. Because acid rain does not respect national boundaries, it creates international problems.[13]

The burning of fossil fuels also creates the so-called greenhouse effect. The term itself may be confusing to children who take it literally and imagine that greenhouses are causing air pollution. The "greenhouse effect" is a metaphor for a situation that human beings have created — the release into the atmosphere of carbon dioxide, nitrous oxide, methane (natural gas), and other substances that form layers of gases, "the exhaling breath of the industrial culture upon which our civilization rests."[14] The layers of gases trap heat, much as the window panes in a greenhouse do, instead of allowing the heat to escape into space. The result is an increase in average temperatures around the globe. Scientists have used computer models to predict the results of global warming: flooding of coastlines as a result of the melting of glaciers and the polar ice caps; widespread crop reduction as a result of drought; soil erosion, desertification, and decrease in rainfall due to the loss of trees. Not everyone agrees with these predictions, but environmentalists believe that there is cause for alarm. Bill McKibben, author of *The End of Nature*, says, "The choice of doing nothing — of continuing to burn ever more oil and coal — is not a choice.... It will lead us, if not straight to hell, then straight to a place with a similar temperature."[15]

A third global problem related to atmospheric pollution is the destruction of the ozone layer. Ozone, a form of oxygen molecule made up of three oxygen atoms, blocks much of the sun's ultraviolet radiation, which causes skin cancer in humans and various kinds of damage and mutations in animals and plants. A "hole" in the ozone layer, such as the one that has been detected over Antarctica, is caused by the attack on ozone of chlorine atoms, which are released by the use of chlorofluorocarbons (CFCs). CFCs are used in manufacturing polystyrene products, which are usually called styrofoam (a trademark of Dow Chemical). They are also released when styrofoam products are burned. They are used in refrigerators and air conditioners, including automobile air conditioners, and as propellants in aerosol cans.[16]

Only one of the "three R's" can provide solutions to the problems of contamination of the atmosphere: reducing our use of fossil fuels and of CFCs. Styrofoam can by recycled into such products as trays and insulation material, but it does not decompose in an ecologically sound way once it's discarded. CFCs can be recaptured from leaky air conditioners in cars and during repairs on refrigerators, but mechanics and repair service personnel may need to be asked to do so. As yet, nothing can be done to recapture CFCs once they are released into the atmosphere by manufacturing or incinerating processes.

The United States is the largest generator of carbon dioxide, the major cause of air pollution. Automobiles in the United States contribute one billion tons of carbon dioxide to the atmosphere every year. Do any of us really need to drive ourselves to work or to school? What would happen if communities insisted that children could be transported to school only by bus? What would happen if teenagers had to take public transportation to their after-school jobs? How many of them would need jobs if they didn't have an automobile habit to support?

Another "R" is one answer to the problem of carbon dioxide pollution: reforestation. Trees absorb carbon dioxide and some particulates that are components of urban air pollution. They also provide shade that reduces the need for pollution-causing air conditioners. A single forest tree absorbs twenty-six pounds of carbon dioxide a year; all the forests in the United States can remove more than 1.7 billion tons of carbon dioxide a year.[17]

But planting trees cannot be the only solution. Each year, the burning of fossil fuels produces about 5.6 billion tons of carbon dioxide. The only sure solution to the problem of air pollution is reduction of our use of pollution producers. This will require the development and use of safe and renewable forms of energy, such as power from wind and water and from solar power stored in solar collectors and photovoltaic cells,[18] in the near future. For the long term, development of safe nuclear technology may be a solution, although nuclear accidents such as those at Chernobyl and Three Mile Island continue to raise questions about the feasibility of this form of energy.

For the present, reduction in consumption of nonrenewable forms of energy means a change in lifestyle for almost everyone in the world. As Bill McKibben notes, "carbon dioxide and the other greenhouse gases come from everywhere, so they can be fixed only by fixing everything."[19] Lester Brown, president of the Worldwatch Institute, is more specific about what this means: "Materialism simply cannot survive the transition to a sustainable world."[20]

The Problem of Managing Water Resources

In the United States, we tend to take the availability of clean water for granted. In much of the world, however, people must use the same water supply for drinking, cooking, cleaning, bathing, irrigation, care of livestock, and waste disposal. The result is that twenty-five million people, 60 percent of them children, die annually from causes related to polluted water. About two-thirds of the world's population does not have access to clean water.[21]

Pollution of streams, rivers, and oceans is caused by a number of factors: agricultural runoff, including fertilizers and toxic pesticides; sewage; industrial wastes; dumping of garbage; oil spills; deliberate alterations of aquatic ecosystems that result in waterways choked by algae. In addition, groundwater, the source of drinking water for more than half the people in the United States, can be polluted by the dumping of toxic wastes in landfills, which leach into underground water supplies.

When an oil tanker dumps millions of gallons of its cargo on a coastal shoreline, or when medical wastes wash up on beaches intended for recreational activities, everyone becomes aware that we are treating our oceans as giant garbage disposals. Yet few of us think about the wastes that we dispose of every day through household drainage systems. The same products that remove stains from our laundry add polluting phosphates to the waste water. Many household cleaners contain harsh chemicals that pollute the environment when they are flushed down drains or when containers are discarded. Most of these products can be replaced by natural, nontoxic substances such as soapflakes and washing soda (instead of detergent), vinegar or borax (instead of chlorine or ammonia products), baking soda (instead of chemical deodorizers), lemon or linseed oil and beeswax (instead of furniture polish), and fuller's earth (instead of chemical spot removers).

Every household in the United States contributes to the depletion and pollution of our water resources. No one can be expected to stop using water. But everyone can be expected to practice the three R's. Reduce unnecessary consumption of water. Reuse household waste water whenever possible to water plants or rinse outdoor surfaces such as patios and walkways. (If it doesn't contain harsh chemicals, it won't harm plants.) Contribute to the safe recycling of water by refraining from contaminating sewer systems with toxic substances. The idea is to return water to the hydrologic cycle, the process by which water is exchanged between the soil and the atmosphere by absorption and transpiration, in as pure a state as possible.

Efforts to care for the earth's water resources go beyond household concerns. Almost every community is affected by local treatment of wetlands — swamps, marshes, bogs, and just about any piece of real estate that collects water and supports an aquatic ecosystem. For most of our history, we have regarded wetlands as wastelands because they are difficult to develop.

More than half of our national wetlands have been "developed," mostly for farming, since Europeans first arrived in North America. Now we are discovering that filling in our wetlands may not be such a good idea.

Wetlands are important to our water supply for a number of reasons. Besides supporting great varieties of vegetation and wildlife, they protect shorelines and reduce inland flooding by slowing and storing flood waters. They reduce pollution by purifying waters that pass through them. They refill underground aquifers. They hold water during wet seasons of the year and release it during dry seasons so that streams can maintain a steady flow. They also emit and absorb gases that help to maintain the planet's atmospheric balance.[22]

When wetlands are filled in and paved over, a community can begin to experience flooding. Concrete doesn't absorb water. Filling in wetlands to create farmland can also cause problems, since wetlands are complex ecosystems whose myriad functions are destroyed by the conversion.

In the Third World, many of the "natural disasters" related to watersheds are in fact unnatural disasters caused by human alteration of the aquatic ecosystems. Deforestation, in particular, causes soil erosion, which leads to silting of rivers that causes flooding. The catastrophic floods that occurred in 1988 in Bangladesh originated in the Himalayan watershed of the Ganges River system. People who live in Bhutan, India, Nepal, and Tibet have stripped the land of wood for fuel, reducing the soil's ability to hold water. The result is that the normal flow of water and silt from these regions, necessary for the sustenance of agriculture in Bangladesh, increased to the point where excessive amounts of both overwhelmed the low-lying country. As a result of the environmental devastation, millions of people were left homeless and thousands became ill or died because of contaminated water supplies.[23]

As the floods in Bangladesh illustrate, threats to the balance of the earth's water systems cross national boundaries. Pollution caused by chemicals, sewage, and deforestation is everyone's problem.

The Problems of Land Devastation

Ecosystems are interdependent, and many of the problems that affect air and water resources originate from land-based activities.

Deforestation has already been mentioned as a cause of both global warming and flooding. It is also a cause of degradation of the land in many parts of the world.

The clearing of forests in the First World is usually the result of industrial activities: the harvesting of wood products for building materials and the manufacturing of other consumables. (It has been estimated that the production of one edition of the Sunday *New York Times* uses some seventy-five thousand trees!)[24] In the Third World, deforestation is usually a matter of survival.

Many indigenous peoples in the Third World practiced sustainable methods of agriculture until the twentieth century. They were often herders, farmers, or hunters who held land in common, shared their resources, and practiced environmentally responsible methods of growing crops. In some cases, technology meant to improve their living standards, like the introduction of hybrid seeds and chemical fertilizers as part of the so-called Green Revolution of the 1950s, has resulted instead in poverty and environmental degradation. In the Third World, the two go hand in hand.

Agricultural methods introduced to the Third World in the twentieth century did increase food supplies, but they also introduced debt to Third World farmers. Green Revolution methods required the purchase of fertilizers and pesticides, as well as new seed supplies each year, since the new high-yielding varieties of seeds could not be stored and replanted from year to year. A single crop failure for many farmers meant the loss of land because of accumulated debt.[25]

Landless farmers must struggle to survive. They will simply move on when land is exhausted because they lack the resources to renew spent soil. They will practice "slash-and-burn" farming to clear forests for farmland when necessary. Animal dung that might be used for fertilizer must be dried and used for fuel instead when trees are no longer available for fuel. Such deforestation and depletion of the soil result in erosion, desertification, and warming of the atmosphere. They also contribute to the growing population of refugees who are constantly on the move in search of survival.

The destruction of rain forests around the world, particularly in the Amazon regions, is a good example of the complexity and interconnectedness of environmental issues. Much of the destruction is occurring because of First World demands on this Third World resource. The United States imports almost eight hundred million pounds of paper from Brazil, where pulp mills process trees cut from the rain forests.[26] The trees are also cut down to make land available for the grazing of cattle to meet the demand for meat exports for U.S. consumption in fast food outlets — the so-called hamburger connection. The destruction of the rain forests is particularly unfortunate, because, unlike other kinds of forests, they are not renewable. You can replant a pine forest; you cannot replant a rain forest. To add to the catastrophe, once the forest is cut down, the quality of the soil diminishes quickly, since it is the trees in the forest that contain nutrients, not the soil. The loss of trees contributes to the increase of carbon dioxide in the atmosphere. Indigenous peoples who have lived in harmony with the forests for centuries are driven from their lands. Many of them fall ill because of exposure to diseases introduced by loggers and other representatives of another civilization with whom they now come into contact.

The U.S. appetite for consumption of resources not only creates problems as a result of demand, but also creates problems of disposal. We have already seen that pouring wastes into the atmosphere and into streams, rivers, and oceans causes environmental problems. The land does not escape these problems either. We dump our solid wastes into landfills, which are rapidly filling up, or pay to have our garbage hauled elsewhere — anywhere, so long as it's NIMBY ("Not In My Back Yard"). The problem with landfills is that they don't go away. Much of what gets dumped in them doesn't decompose, even when the materials are biodegradable, because landfill management does not create conditions which allow for decomposition, such as access to sunlight, oxygen, or water flow. Because of the instability of the fill, landfills are not considered desirable for reuse. (Would you want to build a house on layers of disposable diapers? Would you want your children to go to a school situated on a mountain of styrofoam cartons?)

Toxic wastes pose a particular problem because of their threat to health and safety. Some companies have tried to solve the problem of disposal of toxic wastes by paying Third World countries to accept them for storage — an extreme example of the NIMBY syndrome.

Most of us will admit that we contribute something to the problem of solid waste disposal, but we tend to insist that our contributions are minimal compared to the total volume of trash and garbage. Harried parents who rely on the convenience of disposable diapers point out that they constitute only 2 percent of landfill garbage. This doesn't sound like much until you consider that the diapers won't degrade for three hundred to five hundred years. That's a rather permanent 2 percent. Not to mention the twenty-one million trees and seventy-five thousand metric tons of plastic that go annually into the production of the diapers, which are bleached by a process that emits toxic dioxins.[27]

So what's a mother (or father) to do? If we apply the three R formula to the diaper dilemma, the answers are fairly obvious: reduce the use of disposables if you can't eliminate them entirely; reuse cloth diapers; recycle old diapers when you're finished with them by using them for cleaning rags (instead of using paper products or sponges).

The same formula applies to everything we consume. Discarded paper (including newspapers) makes up about 37 percent of what goes into landfills. Yard wastes account for 20 percent of the garbage we produce in the United States.[28] Even though these materials are "biodegradable," they won't decompose in landfills where they cannot be exposed to oxygen, light, and water flow. Other materials labeled "biodegradable" may not decompose for the same reasons, at least not for several generations. The best answer to the problem of landfills is to prevent waste from arriving at them in the first place. This approach is called "source reduction" by environmentalists, and it means that we reduce the quantity of things we discard.

Ask children to imagine how their behavior would change if they had to dispose of their trash or garbage somewhere in their own neighborhood. In order to avoid turning their back yards into Mount Trashmores, they would find ways to practice the three R's. They would become more aware of the subtle ways that patterns of consumption are shaped by advertising and marketing. For example, the fashion industry creates a "need" to buy new clothes and discard perfectly usable ones every season. Teenagers are particularly susceptible to the temptation to keep up with the latest fads. Throwaway products and packaging contribute enormous amounts of trash to the environment. (Elaborate packaging, besides making a product more attractive, also prevents shoplifting by increasing the size of small, easily-hidden products. Shoplifting is not just a crime; it's an environmental insult.)

Many organizations are working to raise awareness of environmental problems and to get people involved in doing something about them. Children may enjoy learning about their activities. These "green" groups range from educational centers like the National Wildlife Federation to Greenpeace and Earth First!, which are more activist in their orientation. In Europe, there are even "green" political parties to shape the environmental agenda at the government level.

Global awareness leads to the realization that the world is our back yard. As a result, we learn to "lighten our load on the earth" so that we don't pollute and destroy the home that belongs to all of us. Children are never too young to learn environmental lessons. They will learn them effectively through the consistent examples of parents and teachers who model environmentally responsible lifestyles.

Summary

The most important issue of global awareness facing our children is the fate of the environment. The industrialization of First World countries and the poverty of Third World countries are causing the destruction of the air, water, and land resources of our planet to a degree that ultimately threatens the existence of future generations. For the Christian, care for creation is a moral imperative. For all people, it must be a matter of concern since we are all connected by ecological systems.

Acid rain, the destruction of the ozone layer, and the greenhouse effect all threaten our atmospheric resources. Pollution of rivers, streams, and oceans from a number of sources threatens the health and livelihood of two-thirds of the world's population. Land resources are being devastated by deforestation and the accumulation of nondegradable trash. Third World countries suffer the ill effects of both the consumption of raw materials and the disposal of waste products by First World countries.

The solutions to environmental problems can be summed up by the three R's: reduce, reuse, recycle. Children can and must be taught to reduce consumption of resources, reuse whatever materials they can, and recycle materials that can no longer be used. These imperatives fall under the heading of the big R: personal responsibility for the fate of the earth.

Chapter 8

Teaching Awareness: Development, Debt, Discrimination

∾

TEACHING ABOUT THE ROOTS of poverty in Third World countries is a complex undertaking. It's understandable that very few people feel competent to take on the subject. It's easy to assume that people in the Third World are poor for the same reasons people in the United States are poor: they are uneducated or jobless or they just "slipped through the cracks."

It's important that we not let children grow up with that assumption. They may acquire the attitudes expressed by one student who wrote to our office that "people in third world countries have never tried to do anything for themselves. That includes growing food and setting up shelter." Then, pointing a finger at the work we do, our critic continued: "Why should they! They know other people like you will do all the work for them."[1] If our limited resources were multiplied considerably, that might begin to be a possibility — but it's not now! Even if it were, most people in Third World countries would rather direct their own destinies than rely on people in other countries for their subsistence.

People in Third World countries are not poor for the same reasons people in First World countries are poor. Furthermore, they are doing more to help themselves than most children can imagine. This chapter will discuss briefly the reasons for Third World poverty and appropriate ways for children to respond to the needs of the people of the Third World.

Any attempt to explain a complex economic situation in a few paragraphs is bound to be simplistic. For someone who views the situation from a particular faith perspective, it will also be biased.

Having confessed my lack of objectivity, I encourage you to read further on this issue in order to make your own judgments and develop your own perspectives.

The Origins of Third World Debt

Following World War II, three institutions were formed as a means of avoiding the types of international economic chaos that had followed World War I: the General Agreement on Tariffs and Trade (GATT), the International Monetary Fund (IMF), and the World Bank. GATT's work was to reduce tariffs in order to promote free trade. As trade flourished, transnational corporations grew. The IMF was established as part of the United Nations system to manage the exchange rate system and to make short-term loans to countries that had temporary balance-of-payment problems. The World Bank was set up to promote growth and development, primarily in the Third World.[2]

The economic model for these institutions was based on First World market economies. The development programs they promoted were imposed on Third World countries with no experience of First World economic systems. While people in the Third World had traditionally practiced sustainable development, the newly introduced models of development promoted massive borrowing, new technologies, and heavy exporting of goods and services, often at the expense of the needs of the population.[3]

One example of this kind of development is the so-called Green Revolution, which began in the 1950s. Its purpose was to increase the yield of subsistence farmers so that they would have cash crops to sell. The new high-yield seeds had to be purchased each year as did the fertilizers required to grow them. (Farmers had previously saved seeds to plant from their crops and had rotated crops in order to replenish nutrients in the soil. This method of farming did not require purchasing seeds or fertilizer.) In order to join the "Green Revolution," farmers had to borrow money to purchase seeds and fertilizer. All went well so long as growing conditions were favorable. But one failed crop would leave a farmer in debt. Because the hybrid seeds were not indigenous to the regions in which they were grown, crop failure was not uncommon. Fluctuations in the price and availability of fertilizer could also add to the problem, as the seeds would not grow without it and the farmer might have to take on additional debt to purchase it. Farmers who fell too far into debt lost their land to their debtors and were left without collateral for further loans.[4]

Imagine this mini-scenario on a national or global scale, and you have some idea of how Third World debt developed. During the 1970s, money from the profits of oil-exporting countries was deposited in multinational banks, which then were able to make development loans to Third World countries. In the 1980s, some of these countries began to default on payments of their enormous debts for a number of reasons, including falling commodity prices. Various solutions were proposed by First World institutions, among them the so-called Structural Adjustment Programs (SAPs). These involve severe austerity measures imposed by national governments, such as reducing spending for social services, devaluing currency, reducing wages, and cutting imports. The result is great political unrest among the people who suffer deprivation.

To make matters worse, much of the debt in some countries cannot be accounted for. About half of the funds went to infrastructure projects such as roads, dams, and power plants (some of which damaged the environment and displaced the people who lived there) or to the purchase of arms and the buildup of military industries. The rest went to bank accounts or the purchase of real estate in "safe" countries by the ruling elite.[5]

Loans for these "development" projects are being repaid with the lives of the poor.

Because, in part, of these evidences of corruption in government, the IMF and World Bank have begun to press Third World governments to liberalize both their economies and their politics. Particularly in Africa, democracy and pluralism are being suggested as solutions to economic problems. Africa, however, has no tradition of democracy. It does have a long tradition of rule by elites.

One of the legacies of colonialism is the lack of nationalism in most countries. Boundaries were arbitrarily determined, with the result that ethnic and tribal loyalties cross national boundaries. Zaire, for example, has two hundred ethnic groups.[6] Political parties, if established, could be expected to develop according to ethnic, rather than national, loyalties. Models of development that have "worked" in the industrialized First World do not necessarily fit the unindustrialized Third World.

Many non-governmental organizations (NGOs) that work with

the people of the Third World claim that the root of the debt crisis is the Western model of development imposed on Third World countries, usually without consultation with the people affected by development projects. The exclusion of local communities from the planning, implementation, and maintenance of local projects has had disastrous results. For example, a missionary in Kapanda, Zambia, reports that a diesel engine, acquired by the local agricultural project "on loan" to activate a mill to grind corn, is broken, and no one can repair it or pay for repairs. Next to the engine room are stored thousands of bags of corn, which are slowly being destroyed by mice, rats, and the elements. Such examples of mismanagement "can be multiplied indefinitely all over the rural area," he says.[7]

In the town of El Cedro in the Dominican Republic, the 1970s were a time of relative prosperity. Due to high world sugar prices, the local economy was booming. The road was paved, power lines reached the town, and a filtration plant pumped clean water into the town. A health clinic and a school were planned.

In 1990, the road needs repairs, electrical service is unpredictable, and the pump is broken. No one in El Cedro knows how to fix these problems. Once again, people both bathe in and drink from the river. Even though they enjoy a political freedom that they didn't have in the 1970s, the people are struggling to reverse their economic decline. They have learned that political freedom does not necessarily mean prosperity.[8]

When people are involved in making the decisions that affect their lives, their investment in the outcome of the decisions will be high. When they are told what to do and how to run their lives with little or no consultation, they don't learn how to take responsibility for their lives. We have seen that that is true for the way children learn. It is also true of adult learning.

Discrimination: An Impediment to Development

Nowhere has the paternalistic model of development been more devastating than in the lives of women in the Third World. Although First World women are still struggling to overcome sexist attitudes on many levels, they do not face the same kinds of cultural and historical oppression that women in the Third World still endure.

In no country in the world does the Gross National Product take into account the work of volunteers, most of whom are women, or the labors of women in the home. In the entire world, the value of this work is estimated to be four trillion dollars, or about one-third of the present value of the world's economic product.[9] The GNP also does not take into account the economic losses caused by pollution and natural resource depletion — a major factor contributing to unsound economic practices.[10] The degradation of both women and the environment are further linked by the fact that the desperation of impoverished women is contributing to the depletion of scarce resources. In most Third World countries, women are the primary users of the environment, since they are the ones who provide the fuel, food, and water for their families. But, as a report of the United Nations Population Fund notes, "the current state of the relationship between women and the natural environment is a crushing indictment of society's attitude to both. Until new values are attached, their joint degradation will continue."[11]

Women and Hunger

Forty percent of the world's hungry are children; most of the rest are women.[12] One-third of Third World families are headed by women.[13] Sixty to eighty percent of all agricultural work in Africa is done by women. In addition to growing and selling or exchanging food, they are responsible for grinding it, collecting fuel and water, and cooking the food.[14] Yet women are routinely excluded from planning for agricultural development projects.

This can be a costly mistake. A report from the Agency for International Development's (AID) Northeast Rainfed Agricultural Development project in Thailand illustrates the problem:

> Project management assumed that men were the principal farmers and trained them to carry out crop trials. In reality, many men had outside income sources and were frequently away from the farm. Because wives of farmers received no training, crops were planted incorrectly and did not grow, the power tillers provided by the project could not be used, and a nitrogen-fixing crop intended to fertilize rice did not get planted. Women were never consulted about their interest in the project.[15]

In agricultural development projects where machinery is introduced in activities traditionally done by women, men take over the women's jobs. When cash crops, crops raised for export or sale in cities, are cultivated, they are generally grown by men, although the weeding is left to the women because it is considered women's work. Raising subsistence crops, those the family lives on, is the work of women. Cash crops are allotted the best soil; subsistence crops must be raised on what land is left. When women sell any surplus from crops, or any handicrafts they may make, they tend to spend the extra income on their families.[16] The same is not true of men. Since most women's work is unpaid, they have no collateral and no way to obtain loans.

To add to their oppression, women in Third World countries are often excluded from educational opportunities on the grounds that they don't need education. Two-thirds of the people in the world who are illiterate are female. Yet when women in Kenya, who run 38 percent of the farms, were given the same level of help as men, they were more efficient and produced bigger harvests.[17]

All over the Third World, women are banding together in co-operative organizations to better their lives. In many places, they are leaders in environmental movements because they realize that the fate of their families is directly related to the fate of the environment.

The Chipko Movement was born in 1973 in the Garhwal hills of Uttar Pradesh, India, when a timber company threatened the woods above the village. Women played a key role in preventing the logging operations by hugging ("chipko" means "hug") the trees and daring the loggers to strike them.[18] Even today, the term "tree huggers" is used to label environmental activists.

In Kenya, under the leadership of Wangari Maathai, the first woman professor in Kenya, women have planted over 250 "green belts," which reduce the need for rural migration. They establish nurseries for fast-growing trees, raise nitrogen-fixing plants to enrich the soil, and replenish wood that is cut for fuel.[19]

In Bangladesh, Muhammad Yunus believes that economic development for women is a human right. He is founder and managing director of the Grameen Bank, which has 690,000 landless members. The bank makes loans to women who need credit to build their own lives with their own labor. In a typical month, the bank lends in excess of six million dollars, and more than 90 percent of that amount goes to women. The repayment rate is 98 percent.[20]

When women begin to take charge of their lives, they exhibit enormous resourcefulness and perseverance. The potential development of women's capabilities is an untapped resource that promises hope for Third World countries.

The Question of Population

Almost any discussion of women and development raises the issue of population growth. Research has shown that meaningful opportunities for education and employment, along with lower infant mortality rates, will cause fertility rates to decline.[21] Poor women bear large numbers of children because they know that some of them will die before they reach adulthood.

Children are a blessing to overworked Third World women, an extra pair of hands to help with the endless work of survival. Worldwide, women work twice as many hours as men.[22] Furthermore, their work begins early.

Little girls who make dolls out of clay more often than not have a real baby sister or brother to carry on their backs just as soon as they are old enough to bear the load. Girls are often kept out of school, if there is one, because they are needed to help with the work at home. Girls who take on such responsibilities early in life miss out on the chance to be children and, especially, to do the real work of children, which is play.

Mothers and Children

When women suffer from oppression, their children suffer, too. Mothers who are exhausted and malnourished cannot provide the stimulation and the nutrition that their children need to grow into healthy adults. Children who are malnourished from infancy will lack the energy to play and to learn, should they have the opportunity to learn. They are destined to grow into adults with limited options for employment and for supporting children of their own. So the cycle of poverty continues.

Fifteen million small children die from hunger-related causes every year.[23] It's hard to teach children the magnitude of that number. One way to bring such astronomical sums down to earth is to help children to think about them in proportion to a number they can visualize, like the number of children in their class or the number of children in the school. If there are three hundred children in your school, the number of children who die from hunger each year is equivalent to fifty thousand schools like yours. Even that number is hard to comprehend.

Children in Third World countries die of diseases that are easily managed and cured in First World countries. They die because their undernourished bodies cannot withstand infections that would not kill First World children. They die because there isn't enough money for vaccines. They die of dehydration because their mothers don't know how to treat diarrhea.

Responding to Third World Dilemmas

Children have generous hearts and will respond instinctively to pictures of forlorn, hungry, and tattered children, particularly if the appeal is to an emergency situation. If we give them the impression that this is a sufficient reaction, we are cheating them of the truth.

The truth is that the poor know better than we do what they need for themselves. Given the means, they can provide for themselves. What they lack are the conditions to satisfy the basic rights to which every human being is entitled. They do not want charity. They do need justice to ensure those rights. They need access to means of producing food in a sustainable way. They need education. They need medical care. They have the right to the satisfaction of these needs because they are human beings and for no other reason. We who have the means to satisfy our needs and much, much more are required by the demands of justice to see that justice is done.

Fund-raising appeals that depict the people of the Third World as pitiful and needy do not do justice. It is true that there are children with stick limbs and swollen bellies and adults with hollow eyes and fly-swept faces. But they are not the norm. The Third World is not a perpetual disaster zone. The people of the Third World are dignified, industrious individuals who are working harder than any relief agency is to better themselves. That is the first lesson we need to teach our children.

When they respond in charity to appeals for help, children should be taught to ask themselves whose needs are being met by "adoption" plans or crisis-centered approaches designed to make the donor feel good by "putting a face" on the appeal. Less personal are appeals by organizations that direct funds to long-term efforts like schools, clinics, agricultural programs, and self-help projects. Children should be able to distinguish between "relief" and "development" appeals and to make informed choices about how their donations are being used.

The second lesson children need to learn is the hard truth that First World consumerism is contributing to Third World poverty. Food and resources that could be used to sustain Third World families are being exported to the First World to meet demands created by consumer societies. Third World governments need to export more than they import if they are going to be able to repay the enormous debts they have accrued at the urging of First World development planners.

Ask children to imagine how they would feel if they were forced to give most of their weekly allowance to a friend (?) who had sold them a CD player, on credit and with no guarantees, that broke down before it was paid for. Should they pay off the whole debt? Should Third World countries pay off debts for programs that haven't improved the lives of their people?

Where Does the Money Go?

The third and most difficult lesson we must teach our children about development economics is that we are responsible for the way our investment money is used. Does your child have a savings account? What does the bank do with his or her money? Are you vested in a pension fund? How is the fund's money invested? How does your worshipping congregation choose criteria for investing your offerings? Do you or your child own a savings bond or a certificate of deposit? Do you pay taxes? How are these funds used? Do you know?

"Socially responsible" investment plans offer an opportunity to choose responsible criteria for personal and corporate investments. They deserve investigation.[24]

For most of us, the mysteries of the world of finance seem incomprehensible. Yet, it is our money, the accumulated dollars of many small investors, that is financing some portion of what is happening in the Third World, for good or for ill. We owe it to ourselves and to our children to learn the basics of economics so that we can teach our children criteria for responsible investment.[25]

Some Lessons to Learn

People who suffer disadvantage or oppression learn to deal with ambiguity and contradiction. They learn to see the world from multiple points of view. Reduced to nothing, they know the meaning of initiative — and of hope. All of these characteristics are evidences of moral maturity. Our children can find some role models for growing in truth in the lives of some people in the Third World.

Summary

Development, debt, and discrimination are all dimensions of the roots of poverty in the Third World. Children need to learn at least the basics about these realities so that they will not assume that people in the Third World are incapable of providing for themselves.

The heavy burden of debt that Third World countries now carry is the result of development initiatives that began in the years following World War II. Many of these initiatives failed because they applied First World methods of development to Third World environments where they were not suitable. In addition, Third World countries have a long history of colonialism and rule by elites and have no experience of democratic institutions.

Women suffer a particular burden of discrimination in the Third World. They are excluded from education and from economic assistance, although they do much of the agricultural work. When women suffer, their children also suffer. Children in the Third World die of conditions that are easily treated in the First World.

Teaching children to respond to these dilemmas begins with their realization that people in the Third World can solve their own problems if their basic human needs are met. Children also need to learn that First World consumerism is contributing to Third World poverty. Finally, children need to learn the basics of economic theory so that they can grow into adults who are able to make socially responsible investments.

Chapter 9

Heading Where We Want to Go

~

WHEN WE NEED A SUCCINCT WORD OF WISDOM, we refer to Chinese proverbs. Here's one that suits the theme of this chapter: "If we do not change our direction, we are likely to end up where we are headed."

Most of us don't like change. Psychologists say that's because we fear the unknown. I think there's another, simpler reason. Change means taking the time to learn something new, and most of us don't have the time to spare. We are too busy making it from one end of the day to the other. Taking the time to read the newspaper, or sitting down to figure out how to infuse an entire curriculum with global awareness, just doesn't seem feasible.

Yet most of us know that the direction in which we're now headed doesn't look too promising. If we don't change the way our children are learning about the world, we are wasting our educational energies. We need to head in a different direction, and that means changing the orientation of our lives.

Laying Down Our Lives

Whenever I hear the passage in John's Gospel about proving one's love by laying down one's life, I wonder what kind of a lover I would be if I were called on to die for my children. Most people familiar with that passage think of it in terms of dying for a loved one. But a young mother gave me a new perspective on that passage. "I lay down my life for my children every day," she said. "I put aside what I am doing to answer their questions with my full attention. When I am playing with them or teaching them something, I concentrate on them."

How we spend our time teaches our children what we value. Just as we spend time learning things that are important to us, children are willing to spend time learning about things that are important to them.

Spending time to teach children to care about the fate and the feelings of other people is one way to get them headed in the direction of global awareness. If children learn to care about the world and the people in it, they will have the motivation to learn what they need to know to be global citizens.

If we value global awareness education, we may need to lay down our lives for our children. We may need to spend some time learning about global realities and giving our children opportunities to experience them.

A Matter of Values

Much of the material in this book has focused on the situation of people in the Third World. Since my concern is global awareness education that raises consciousness of the needs of the oppressed, my perspective is shaped by that concern. If you are concerned with the role of the United States in the world economy, you will approach the task of global awareness education from a different perspective. The children you are raising or teaching will be shaped by your perspective.

First, the Bad News

If you believe that you are incapable of doing anything about the state of the world, then your children will believe that, too.

If you regard the destruction of the earth as someone else's problem, then so will your children. (Soon enough, it will be their problem.)

If you permit children to express ethnic, racist, or sexist bias without any comment from you, they will grow up to be bigots who will have trouble living and working in a pluralistic society.

If you believe that participation in the decisions that shape your life and the lives of your children is beyond your abilities, then it will be — and your children will learn that they are powerless.

It all depends on where you're headed and whether or not you want to change directions.

The Good News

People who have had the experience of being powerless but have persisted in struggling to gain control over their lives have an important lesson to teach us. The lesson is that individuals can make change happen when they join their efforts, in trust and in hope, with other like-minded individuals. At the very least, they can say "no" to anything that's going in the wrong direction.

The theories of quantum physics tells us that change happens when you have enough pockets of energy in the right places. Sometimes it takes one person to light the spark that ignites the smaller efforts and turns them into a global one. Rosa Parks, who refused to sit in the back of an Alabama bus, ignited the energy of thousands of people sympathetic to the civil rights movement. Ryan White, who died at eighteen of AIDS, taught us all, with grace and dignity in the face of fear, not to be afraid of what we don't understand.

We may not be able to be Rosa Parks or Ryan White, but we can be part of one of the pockets of energy that can ignite to make the world a better place. The proliferation of private voluntary organizations (PVOs) provides us plenty of opportunity to make connections with people who share our concerns.

We can start by choosing one thing that needs attention. Perhaps something in this book raised questions that invite further exploration of an issue.

We can decide to learn more about ways to save the environment — and then practice them. We can find out more about the financial systems in which we have investments — and figure out ways to teach our children how to assess them. We can make an effort to plan leisure activities that put us in touch with public life. We can look over our lesson plans for the next month and devise ways to incorporate global awareness into the lessons.

We can practice conflict resolution skills whenever the occasion arises. We can try cooperative learning styles in the classroom. We can think about cooperative ways of doing things, like recycling trash, in the neighborhood.

Or we can do nothing. Inertia is easier.

Please don't choose inertia.

A Success Story

If you think that ordinary people can't make much difference when it comes to teaching children about global awareness, this story is for you.

Once upon a time (actually, about fifty years ago), a young woman and a young man met and fell in love and got married.

They had been raised in a conservative and racist environment, but they decided not to raise their children that way.

They had two daughters and a son. The family wasn't poor, but the bicycles and piano and the family automobiles and some of the furniture were usually second-hand, and books mostly came from the library. There were lots of books and newspapers around (because the parents valued them), and the house was always filled with flowers that were known by name (because the woman grew them).

Although the parents and the children often held different points of view, there was plenty of laughter and good conversation around the dinner table (because different opinions were considered interesting). The children were encouraged to make their own choices as they matured, even though the parents didn't always think they were wise (and sometimes they weren't).

This family never traveled far from home, but the children grew up to be curious about the world and concerned about the people in it. One daughter now works for an international organization that teaches global awareness and raises funds for Third World children. The other daughter, an avid globetrotter, is a teacher and administrator in an international school system that educates children from all over the world. The son, a lawyer, has built a career defending the poor who cannot afford lawyers.

The parents who raised them profess to be mystified by the global consciousness of their children. But people who know my parents are not at all surprised by the careers that my brother and sister and I have chosen.

Thanks, Mom and Dad. You did a great job of teaching us about the world.

I hope that the children you are raising and teaching will say the same to you one day.

Notes

~

Chapter One: Why Teach Global Awareness?

1. See the parable of the good Samaritan, Luke 10:29–37.
2. See "Human Capital: The Decline of America's Work Force," *Business Week*, September 19, 1988, pp. 100–141.
3. Susan Okie, "Health Crisis Confronts 1.3 Billion," *Washington Post*, September 25, 1989, p. A1.
4. Elizabeth M. Fowler, "A New Look at M.B.A. Education," *New York Times*, March 6, 1990, p. D19.
5. Peter Baker, "Va. Colleges Discovering the World," *Washington Post*, January 21, 1990, p. C1.
6. Ibid.
7. Kenneth J. Cooper, "Americans, Soviets Share Symptoms of a Map Gap," *Washington Post*, November 9, 1989, p. A3.
8. Jim Hoagland, "Finally, A Global Economy," *Washington Post*, February 27, 1990, p. A23.
9. Meg Greenfield, "Needed: A New Compass," *Newsweek*, October 2, 1989, p. 80.
10. Clyde V. Prestowitz, Jr., review of *The End of the American Century*, by Steven Schlossten, *New York Times Book Review*, February 18, 1990, p. 24.
11. Sam Roberts, "Japanese Work to Link Business to Philanthropy," *New York Times*, March 12, 1990, p. B1.
12. Neil Henry, "Copter Crew Finds Friends in Ethiopia," *Washington Post*, August 15, 1989.

Chapter Two: What is Global Awareness Education?

1. Elizabeth Brown-Guillory and Lucius M. Guillory, "Demystifying Global Education," *Momentum*, February 1989, p. 58.
2. C. Sny, *Global Education...An Implementation Plan and Resource Guide* (Madison: University of Wisconsin, 1980), p. 3.
3. The Hunger Project, *Ending Hunger: An Idea Whose Time Has Come* (New York: Praeger Publishers, 1985), p. 412.
4. Elizabeth Morgan, *Global Poverty and Personal Responsibility: Integrity through Commitment* (Mahwah, NJ: Paulist Press, 1989), p. 3.
5. *Ending Hunger*, p. 27.

6. American Congress on Surveying and Mapping, *Choosing a World Map: Attributes, Distortions, Classes, Aspects* (Falls Church, VA: American Cartographic Association, 1988), pp. 8–9.

7. Comparisons are taken from the Peters projection produced by the United Nations Development Programme through Friendship Press, P. O. Box 37844, Cincinnati, OH 45237.

Chapter Three: The Content of Global Awareness Education

1. One such organization is CODEL (Coordination in Development), "a consortium of church-related organizations whose primary goal is to provide assistance to self-determined development activities among the socio-economically disadvantaged overseas." For more information, call or write CODEL, 475 Riverside Drive, Room 1842, New York, NY 10115; (212) 870-3000.

2. From "Our Common Future" — Report of the World Commission on Environment and Development (The Brundtland Commission), 1988 in *Renewing the Earth* (London: Catholic Fund for Overseas Development, 1989), p. 12.

3. *Global Realities Fact Sheet*, Catholic Relief Services Global Education Office, Baltimore.

4. Elizabeth Morgan, *Global Poverty and Personal Responsibility: Integrity through Commitment* (Mahwah, NJ: Paulist Press, 1989), p. 50.

5. Patricia Theiler, "Budgeting a 'Peace Dividend,'" *Bread for the World Newsletter*, vol. 2, no. 3 (March 21, 1990), p. 2.

6. *Global Realities Fact Sheet.*

7. *Narrowing the Gap: An Introduction to Third World Poverty and Development Issues*, Catholic Relief Services Global Education Office, Baltimore, p. 28.

8. "Ears to Hear" in *Beyond Familiar Borders*, vol. 1, issue 1 (Spring 1989), Catholic Relief Services Global Education Office, Baltimore.

Chapter Four: Valuing Differences, Making Connections: Attitudes That Promote Global Awareness

1. Rex Nettleford, "A View from the Developing World," address to the 44th Annual Conference of the Association for Supervision and Curriculum Development (Alexandria, VA: ASCD, 1989).

2. Poster displayed by Craig R. Sholley, director, Rwanda Mountain Gorilla Project, quoted by Joanne Omang, "And No Matter What, Don't Beat Your Chest!," *Washington Post*, May 6, 1990, p. E1.

3. Don Oldenburg, "Putting Down Bias," *Washington Post*, March 16, 1990, p. B5.

4. C. G. Jung, *Psychological Types* (Princeton, NJ: Princeton University Press, 1976). The Myers-Briggs Type Indicator is published by the

Consulting Psychologists Press, Inc., 577 College Avenue, Palo Alto, CA 94306.

5. David Keirsey and Marilyn Bates, *Please Understand Me* (Del Mar, CA: Prometheus Nemesis Book Company, 1984), pp. 5–12.

6. George J. Schemel and James A. Borbely, *Facing Your Type* (Wernersville, PA: Typofile Press, 1982), p. 13.

7. Louise Derman-Sparks, *Anti-Bias Curriculum: Tools for Empowering Young Children* (Washington: National Association for the Education of Young Children, 1988), p. 31.

8. Louise Derman-Sparks, "Teaching Children Not to Hate," *Washington Post Education Review*, August 6, 1989, p. 1.

9. Ibid.

10. *Convention on the Rights of the Child* (Geneva: ICCB General Secretariat, 1989), pp. 9–10.

Chapter Five: How Children Learn

1. Constance Kamil and Rheta DeVries, *Group Games in Early Education: Implications of Piaget's Theory* (Washington: National Association for the Education of Young Children, 1980), p. 241.

2. Erik Erikson, *Childhood and Society*, 2nd ed. (New York: Norton, 1963).

3. Erik Erikson, *Insight and Responsibility* (New York: Norton, 1964), pp. 111–57.

4. Lawrence Kohlberg, *The Philosophy of Moral Development: Moral Stages and the Idea of Justice* (New York: Harper & Row, 1981).

5. Elizabeth Morgan, *Global Poverty and Personal Responsibility: Integrity through Commitment* (Mahwah, NJ: Paulist Press, 1989), p. 15.

6. Carol Gilligan, *In a Different Voice* (Cambridge, MA: Harvard University Press, 1982).

Chapter Six: Methods of Teaching Global Awareness

1. Parker Palmer, *The Company of Strangers: Christians and the Renewal of America's Public Life* (New York: Crossroad, 1986), p. 18.

2. Ibid, p. 26.

3. Cosby S. Rogers and Janet K. Sawyers, *Play in the Lives of Children* (Washington: National Association for the Education of Young Children, 1988), p. 3.

4. Ibid., p. 2.

5. Sister Catherine McGrath in a letter to the Holy Childhood Association, May 1990.

6. Sharon Bell Mathis, "John Steptoe: An Artist Remembered," *Washington Post Book World*, May 13, 1990, p. 21.

7. Alison Howard, "Telling Tales in School Is Educational Entertainment," *Washington Post*, February 1, 1990, p. Va.12.

8. Constance Kamil and Rheta DeVries, *Group Games in Early Education: Implications of Piaget's Theory* (Washington: National Association for the Education of Young Children, 1980), pp. 199–200.

9. Cooperative games that teach global awareness are available from Animal Town, P.O. Box 2002, Santa Barbara, CA 93120. On the cover of the Animal Town catalogue is this note: "The concept behind cooperative games is simple. . . . People play with one another rather than against one another; they play to overcome challenges, not to overcome people."

10. Jean Houston, "Whole System Transition: The Birth of Planetary Society," address to the 44th Annual Conference of the Association for Supervision and Curriculum Development (Alexandria, VA: ASCD, 1989).

11. Parker Palmer, *To Know As We Are Known* (San Francisco: Harper & Row, 1983), p. 82.

12. See also the SIGEP approach described by Elizabeth Crary, *Kids Can Cooperate* (Seattle: Parenting Press, Inc., 1984), chapter 4.

13. Ibid., p. 16.

14. "Winning Together," *Maryknoll*, vol. 84, no. 2 (February 1990), p. 35.

15. *Narrowing the Gap: An Introduction to Third World Poverty and Development Issues*, Catholic Relief Services Global Education Office, Baltimore, pp. 16–17. See also "Global Interdependence" in *Make a World of Difference: Creative Activities for Global Learning*, Office on Global Education of the National Council of Churches, Baltimore, p. 63.

16. Robert Muller, "Educating the Global Citizen: Illuminating the Issues," address to the 44th Annual Conference of the Association for Supervision and Curriculum Development (Alexandria, VA: ASCD, 1989). For information about the world core curriculum, write to the Robert Muller School, 6005 Royaloak Drive, Arlington, TX 76016.

17. Contact the Public Information Office of the United Nations, United Nations Plaza, New York, NY 10017. Also contact the United Nations Association of the USA (UNA-USA), an organization working to build support for the United Nations, at 485 Fifth Avenue, New York, NY 10017-6104; (212) 697-3232.

Chapter Seven: Teaching Awareness: The Environment

1. *The United Nations and the Global Environment*, UNA-USA Factsheet, New York, NY, p. 1.

2. Ibid. For more information on the Kenyan Green Belt Movement, write to the National Council of Women of Kenya, P.O. Box 67545, Nairobi, Kenya.

3. Dick Russell, "The Critical Decade — Environmentalism in the

1990's: Where Are We Headed?," *E: The Environmental Magazine*, vol. 1, no. 1, (January/February 1990), p. 35.

4. Ibid., p. 32.

5. To obtain a free copy of *Peace with God the Creator, Peace with All of Creation*, write to the Missionaries of Africa, 1624 21st Street, NW, Washington, DC 20009.

6. Russell, "The Critical Decade — Environmentalism in the 1990's," p. 31.

7. Joseph R. Veneroso, M.M., "No Elephant Joke," *Maryknoll*, vol. 84, no. 2 (February 1990), p. 54.

8. Joanne Omang, review of *Entangling Alliances: How The Third World Shapes Our Lives*, by John Maxwell Hamilton with Nancy Morrison, *Washington Post Book World*, March 25, 1990, p. 7.

9. Elissa Wolfson, ed., "Keeping Ivory on the Elephants," *E: The Environmental Magazine*, vol. 1, no. 1 (January/February 1990), p. 16.

10. Victoria Moran, "Parenting for the Planet," *E: The Environmental Magazine*, vol. 1, no. 1 (January/February 1990), p. 41.

11. Russell, "The Critical Decade — Environmentalism in the 1990's."

12. *Renewing the Earth* (London: Catholic Fund for Overseas Development, 1989), p. 47.

13. Michael G. Renner, "Forging Environmental Alliances," *World Watch*, vol. 2, no. 6 (November/December 1989), p. 10.

14. Al Gore, "Our Global Eco-Blindness," *Washington Post*, May 14, 1989, p. C1.

15. Dennis Drabble, review of *The End of Nature*, by Bill McKibben, *Washington Post Book World*, October 8, 1989, p. 9.

16. Kathy Sawyer, "Rise in Ultraviolet Radiation Tied to Antarctic Ozone Hole," *Washington Post*, April 6, 1989, p. A3.

17. " 'Killer' Trees to the Rescue," *Newsweek*, October 2, 1989, p. 59.

18. Photovoltaic cells make electricity from sunlight. For a report on the use of photovoltaic collectors in Tanzania, see "Harnessing the Sun" by Tim Lyons in *Maryknoll*, vol. 84, no. 2 (February 1990), p. 52.

19. Drabble, review of *The End of Nature*, by Bill McKibben.

20. John Lancaster, " 'Sustainable' Society Urged by Year 2030," *Washington Post*, February 11, 1990.

21. *The United Nations and the Global Environment*, p. 4.

22. William K. Stevens, "Efforts to Halt Wetland Loss Turn Their Attention Inland," *New York Times*, March 13, 1990, p. C12.

23. Jodi L. Jacobson, "Environmental Refugees: A Yardstick of Habitability," Worldwatch Paper 86 (Washington: Worldwatch Institute, 1988), pp. 17–18.

24. Alyssa Burger, ed., "Publishers Make Pledge to Replant Trees," *E: The Environmental Magazine*, vol. 1, no. 1 (January/February 1990), p. 8.

25. See "Indigenous Peoples and the Environment," p. 13, and "Debt and Environment," p. 55, in *Renewing the Earth*.

26. From an advertisement for Earth Care Paper, Inc., Box 3335, Dept. 42, Madison, WI 53704.

27. Linda Chion-Kenney, "The 'Cold Evil': Taking Global Responsibility Personally," *Washington Post*, April 6, 1990, p. C5.

28. Robert J. Samuelson, "The Way We Diaper," *Washington Post*, March 14, 1990.

Chapter Eight: Teaching Awareness: Development, Debt, Discrimination

1. Letter to the National Office of the Holy Childhood Association, October 20, 1989.

2. The Debt Crisis Network, *From Debt to Development* (Washington: Institute for Policy Studies, 1985), pp. 20–22.

3. Brian Jaudon, "The More We Pay, the More We Owe: The Third World Debt Crisis," *Sojourners*, vol. 18, no. 11 (December 1989), p. 9.

4. *Renewing the Earth* (London: Catholic Fund for Overseas Development, 1989), p. 55.

5. *From Debt to Development*, p. 27.

6. Lisa Beyer, "Continental Shift," *Time*, vol. 135, no. 21 (May 21, 1990), p. 36.

7. Reinhold Bloching, M.Afr., "Green Revolution in the Red?" *Justice and Peace*, vol. 3, no. 2 (April–June 1989), p. 2.

8. Al Kamen, "Hope Wears Thin in Dominican Village," *Washington Post*, May 20, 1990, p. A31.

9. *Facts: Children at Risk* (factsheet), Office on Global Education, National Council of Churches.

10. Jeff Martin, "Calculating Real Costs," *Stanley Foundation Courier*, no. 2 (Fall 1989), p. 3.

11. *The United Nations and the Global Environment*, UNA-USA Factsheet, New York, p. 2.

12. The Hunger Project, *Ending Hunger: An Idea Whose Time Has Come* (New York: Praeger Publishers, 1985), p. 14.

13. Lane Vanderslice, *Getting Aid to Women*: Background Paper No. 102 (Washington: Bread for the World, 1988), p. 2.

14. *Facts: Women at Risk* (factsheet), Office on Global Education, National Council of Churches.

15. Vanderslice, *Getting Aid to Women*, p. 4.

16. Ibid., p. 2.

17. *Facts: Women at Risk*.

18. *Renewing the Earth*, p. 60.

19. Ibid.

20. Muhammad Yunus, "Credit as a Human Right," *New York Times*, April 2, 1990, p. A17.

21. Elizabeth Morgan, *Global Poverty and Personal Responsibility: Integrity through Commitment* (Mahwah, NJ: Paulist Press, 1989), p. 48.

22. *Facts: Women at Risk.*

23. *Ending Hunger*, p. 9.

24. See the resource section below, pp. 127–140, for names of some "socially conscious" investment funds.

25. An excellent introduction to economics is *The Study of Economics: Principles, Concepts and Applications*, by Dr. Turley Mings, published by Dushkin Publishing Group, Sluice Dock, Guilford, CT 06437.

Glossary

~

acid rain: atmospheric pollution, caused by the burning of fossil fuels, falling as rain that destroys forests and pollutes bodies of water.

The Brundtland Report (*Our Common Future*): the 1987 report of the World Commission on Environment and Development, which described the relationship between unsound economic activity and environmental degradation.

cash crops: crops grown to be sold for profit.

chauvinism: preference for one's own cause, especially with reference to patriotism.

Cold War: a state of hostility that exists between nations because of ideological, political, or economic differences, but stops short of armed conflict. The term usually refers to the relationship between the United States and the USSR from the period after World War II until the end of the 1980s.

constructivism: the theory proposed by Jean Piaget that holds that children acquire knowledge by interaction with the environment. They "construct" meaning by making connections between objects.

desertification: the process by which arable land becomes desert due to overcultivation, overgrazing, or poor irrigation.

development education: the study of factual information about specific social, economic, and political issues of survival and growth, e.g., hunger, population, and literacy.

empiricism: in educational theory, the thesis that children learn through the senses. Knowledge is external to the child and is poured in by the teacher.

ethnocentrism: focus on one ethnic or cultural identity.

First World: industrialized nations with market economies: those in North America and Western Europe, as well as Australia, New Zealand, and Japan.

fossil fuels: coal, oil, and natural gas (methane), which are derived from fossilized organic matter.

"green" movements: organizations made up of environmental activists, such as Greenpeace and Earth First! In Europe, "the greens" are political parties with an environmental agenda.

greenhouse effect: the release into the atmosphere of carbon dioxide, nitrous oxide, methane. and other gases from the burning of fossil fuels. The layers of gas trap heat instead of allowing it to escape into the atmosphere.

Gross National Product (GNP): the sum of all goods and services produced by a national economy. The GNP does not include the value of unpaid labor, such as that performed in the home, nor does it take into account the depletion of natural resources used to produce goods.

indigenous people: the approximately two hundred million people, nomadic or semi-nomadic, who live in remote areas of the earth, retain distinct cultural heritages, and avoid the mainstream culture, like the Bushmen of southern Africa and the Indians of the Amazon region.

industrialized nations: "developed countries," in which the GNP is derived mainly from industry rather than from agriculture.

infusion: a teaching method for global awareness education by which global information is consciously incorporated into every area of the curriculum in a systematic way.

interdependence: the condition of being connected by political, economic, environmental, and other life systems in such a way that global survival depends on global cooperation.

market economy: "free enterprise" systems in which buyer-seller transactions determine what goods and services are produced.

Mercator projection: a cylindrical map of the world that exaggerates the size of countries in the Northern Hemisphere.

NGOs: nongovernmental organizations, the term used by the United Nations and many countries for nonprofit organizations involved in development issues, particularly those pertaining to the environment and to population growth.

Our Common Future: see Brundtland Report.

Peters projection: a cylindrical map of the world that shows country sizes in correct proportion to one another but distorts their shapes.

preferential option for the poor: human activity that follows the example of Jesus, whose concern for, and identification with, the poor and outcast of society are particular focuses of the Gospels. Pope John Paul II's definition: "a call to have a special oneness with the small and the weak, those that suffer and weep, those that are humiliated and left on the margin of society, so as to help them win their dignity as human persons and children of God."

PVOs: private voluntary organizations, the term commonly used in the United States for nonprofit organizations involved in humanitarian issues and outreach.

rationalism: in educational theory, the thesis that children learn through the innate power of reason. Sensory experience is important to the learning process, but some things cannot be known by the senses.

Robinson projection: an oval map of the world that distorts shapes and sizes in the high latitudes for the sake of showing reasonably correct shapes and proportions at middle and low latitudes.

simulation game: a teaching method for global awareness education by which students experience the cultural situations of other people or the dilemmas people face in solving development problems.

Structural Adjustment Programs (SAPs): stringent economic policies imposed on Third World debtor nations, such as cutting social services, lowering wages, and increasing exports, in order to raise capital to service debts.

subsistence crops: crops grown to feed one's family.

sustainable development: the process by which components of economic growth (e.g., natural resources, technology, investment policies) are managed in such a way that the needs of the present generation are met without endangering the ability of future generations to meet their needs.

Third World: developing nations of Africa, Asia, and Latin America.

Resources for Further Investigation

∽

The following list of resources is by no means exhaustive. Information on every aspect of global awareness education is readily available from many sources. These will help you get started.

Resources are listed by chapters with reference to the topic of each chapter. Some resources may be listed more than once if they deal with more than one topic.

There is a charge or donation requested for most materials. Ask for information when you call or write. Free materials are noted.

Chapter One: Why Teach Global Awareness?

The American Forum for Global Education, 45 John Street, Suite 1200, New York, NY 10038. Nonpartisan, nonprofit organization that develops teaching strategies for global perspectives. Write for information brochure.

Chapter Two: What Is Global Awareness Education?

American Congress on Surveying and Mapping, 210 Little Falls Street, Falls Church, VA 22046. Publishes two technical, but informative, booklets on choosing maps: *Which Map Is Best? Projections for World Maps* (1986) and *Choosing a World Map: Attributes, Distortions, Classes, Aspects* (1988).

Friendship Press, P.O. Box 37844, Cincinnati, OH 45237. Publishes the Peters projection.

The Map Store, 1636 Eye St., NW, Washington, DC 20006; (800) 544-2659. Will provide information on purchasing maps of all kinds, atlases, globes, travel books, items related to geography.

Modern Curriculum Press, 13900 Prospect Road, Cleveland, OH 44136; (800) 321-3106. Publishes maps, charts, graphs, transparencies for use in grades one through eight.

The National Geographic Society, Education Services, Department 90, Washington, DC 20036; (800) 368-2728. Contact for information about all kinds of global awareness educational materials.

PC Globe, Inc., 4700 S. McClintock, Tempe, AZ 85282; (800) 255-2789. Markets an IBM-compatible computerized atlas that features maps and extensive information on government, history, demographics, natural resources and other data. Requires minimum 512 kilobyte memory and color graphics adapter.

Social Studies School Service, 10200 Jefferson Boulevard, Room 6, P.O. Box 802, Culver City, CA 90232-0802. Send for free catalogue of maps, books, videos, posters, computer software, simulation games, transparencies, board games, atlases — in itself an introduction to global awareness.

Chapter Three: The Content of Global Awareness Education

American Youth Work Center, Publications Division, 1751 N Street, NW, Suite 302, Washington, DC 20036. Ask for information about *Covering the Global Village: A Handbook for the Student Press*, a booklet that tells student journalists how to cover Third World issues.

Approvecho Institute, 80574 Hazelton Road, Cottage Grove, OR 97424; (503) 942-9434. Publishes *Skipping Stones*, a multicultural forum for children's essays, letters, and art.

Bread for the World, 802 Rhode Island Avenue, NE, Washington, DC 20018. A Christian advocacy organization that "seeks justice for the world's hungry people by lobbying our nation's decision makers." Publishes well-written analyses of development issues and materials for use by local advocacy groups.

The Catholic Fund for Overseas Development (CAFOD), 2 Romero Close, Stockwell Road, London SW9 9TY, England. Publishes *Renewing the Earth*, an excellent survey, with anecdotes, of development issues. Available from CRS, c/o Postal Church Service, 8401 Southern Boulevard, Youngstown, OH 44512-6798; (216) 758-4545.

Catholic Relief Services, Global Education Office, 209 West Fayette Street, Baltimore, MD 21201; (301) 625-2220. A good source for facts, figures, and anecdotes about Third World development issues. Order materials from CRS/Global Education Office, c/o Postal Church Service, 8401 Southern Boulevard, Youngstown, OH 44512-6798; (216) 758-4545.

CODEL (Coordination in Development), 475 Riverside Drive, Room 1842, New York, NY 10115; (212) 870-3000. A consortium of church-related organizations concerned with development issues in the Third World.

Global Education Associates, 475 Riverside Drive, Suite 456, New York, NY 10115; (212) 870-3290. "An international network of men and women in over 70 countries who conduct research and educational programs aimed at advancing world peace and security, cooperative economic development, human rights, and ecological sustainability."

Holy Childhood Association, 1720 Massachusetts Avenue, NW, Washington, DC 20036; (202) 775-8637. Publishes global awareness, mission education, and fund-raising materials for elementary-age students and their teachers. Free maps and resource guides; free samples of other materials.

Morgan, Elizabeth. *Global Poverty and Personal Responsibility: Integrity through Commitment.* Mahwah, NJ: Paulist Press, 1989. An excellent discussion of the relation between stages of moral development and global responsibility, which recognizes that a sense of global responsibility typically does not develop fully until middle age. Includes useful synopses of basic Third World development issues and proposes strategies for advocacy and action.

National Council of Churches, Office on Global Education, 2115 Charles Street, Baltimore, MD 21218-5755. The NCC is "the primary national expression of the ecumenical movement in the United States." Its members are thirty-two Protestant, Orthodox and Anglican church bodies. Ask for information about publications, especially the Global Education Reprint Series.

The Stanley Foundation, 216 Sycamore Street, Suite 500, Muscatine, IA 52761. Publishes analyses of global issues and reports of conferences on related issues. Write for free copies of *Courier,* an informative newsletter.

World Affairs Materials, Box 726, Kennett Square, PA 19348. Publishes two useful books for introducing development issues to children: *Catching Up with a Changing World* and *Helping Boys and Girls Discover the World* by Leonard S. Kenworthy.

Three publications by missionary organizations are consistently informative with regard to development issues:

> Missionaries of Africa *REPORT*
> 624 21st Street, NW
> Washington, DC 20009-1005

> *Maryknoll Magazine*
> Maryknoll Fathers and Brothers
> Maryknoll, NY 10545

> *Catholic Life*
> PIME Missionaries
> 35750 Moravian Drive
> Fraser, MI 48026

Chapter Four: Valuing Differences, Making Connections: Attitudes That Promote Global Awareness

Association for Supervision and Curriculum Development, 1250 North Pitt Street, Alexandria, VA 22314. Ask for information about global awareness education materials.

International Catholic Child Bureau, c/o ICO Center, 323 East 47th Street, New York, NY 10017; (212) 355-3992. Has available a brochure with the text of the United Nations Convention on the Rights of the Child.

Jung, C. G. *Psychological Types*. Princeton, NJ: Princeton University Press, 1976.

Keirsey, David, and Marilyn Bates. *Please Understand Me*. Prometheus Nemesis Book Company, P.O. Box 2748, Del Mar, CA 92014.

Myers, Isabel Briggs. *Introduction to Type*. Consulting Psychologists Press, Inc., 577 College Avenue, Palo Alto, CA 94306. Booklet that explains the personality type theory on which the Myers-Briggs Type Inventory is based.

National Association for the Education of Young Children, 1834 Connecticut Avenue, NW, Washington, DC 20009; (800) 424-2460. Ask for information about the brochure entitled *Teaching Young Children to Resist Bias: What Parents Can Do* and about the publication *Anti-Bias Curriculum: Tools for Empowering Young Children* by Louise Derman-Sparks.

Schemel, George J., and James A. Borbely. *Facing Your Type*. Typofile Press, Church Road, Box 223, Wernersville, PA 19565. Booklet that uses a "typeface" graphic to demonstrate the concepts and dynamics of type theory.

Chapter Five: How Children Learn

Duska, Ronald, and Mariellen Whelan. *Moral Development: A Guide to Piaget and Kohlberg*. New York: Paulist Press, 1975.

Erikson, Erik. *Childhood and Society*, 2nd ed. New York: Norton, 1963.

Gilligan, Carol. *In a Different Voice*. Cambridge, MA: Harvard University Press, 1982.

Kohlberg, Lawrence. *The Philosophy of Moral Development: Moral Stages and the Idea of Justice*. New York: Harper & Row, 1981.

Moran, Gabriel. *Religious Education Development: Images for the Future*. Minneapolis: Winston Press, 1983.

Morgan, Elizabeth. *Global Poverty and Personal Responsibility: Integrity through Commitment.* Mahwah, NJ: Paulist Press, 1989.

Munsey, Brenda, ed. *Moral Development, Moral Education, and Kohlberg.* Birmingham, AL: Religious Education Press, 1981.

National Association for the Education of Young Children, 1834 Connecticut Avenue, NW, Washington, DC 20009. Send for a catalogue of publications.

Palmer, Parker. *To Know as We Are Known: A Spirituality of Education.* San Francisco: Harper & Row, 1983.

Van Ornum, William, and Mary Wicker Van Ornum. *Talking to Children about Nuclear War.* New York: Continuum, 1984. See the section on developmental concerns in Chapter 4, "Talking Together."

Chapter Six: Methods of Teaching Global Awareness

American Friends Service Committee, 15 Rutherford Place, New York, NY 10003. Send for book list, which includes *The Friendly Classroom for a Small Planet: A Handbook on Creative Approaches to Living and Problem Solving for Children* (1978).

Animal Town Cooperative Ventures, P.O. Box 2002, Santa Barbara, CA 93120. Send for catalogue of cooperative games, including global awareness games.

Association for Supervision and Curriculum Development, 1250 North Pitt Street, Alexandria, VA 22314. Ask for information about tapes of talks from the ASCD 44th Annual Conference in 1989, which focused on global awareness education.

Bessom, Linda, SND de N. *Thumbs Up! Teaching Interdependence to Grades 3 and 4.* Maryknoll Missionaries, Maryknoll, NY 10545, 1989. A series of activities that teach the concept of interdependence by using the thumb.

Catholic Relief Services, Global Education Office, 209 West Fayette Street, Baltimore, MD 21201; (301) 625-2220. Ask for the sixteen-page booklet entitled *Teaching toward Global Understanding and Action,* which contains samples of infused lesson plans.

Center for Teaching International Relations, Publications Department, University of Denver, Denver, CO 80208. Publications "combine teaching methods and learning strategies that actively involve students. Games, role playing, simulations, and case studies are among the various techniques CTIR teaching materials employ." Catalogue includes activity books for elementary, intermediate, and high school levels as well as books on teaching writing and social studies using a global approach.

Childswork/Childsplay, Center for Applied Psychology, 441 North Fifth Street, Philadelphia, PA 19123. Send for catalogue that "addresses the mental health needs of children and their families through play."

Crary, Elizabeth. *Kids Can Cooperate*. Parenting Press, 7750 31st Avenue, NE, Seattle, WA 98115. Strategies for teaching children cooperation, negotiation skills and problem-solving techniques for use both at home and in the classroom.

Derman-Sparks, Louise. *Anti-Bias Curriculum: Tools for Empowering Young Children*. Washington: National Association for the Education of Young Children, 1988. See especially the section on storytelling with "persona" dolls.

Dushkin Publishing Group, Inc., Sluice Dock, Guilford, CT 06437; (800) 243-6532. Publishes high school and college level textbooks, including the Global Studies series that teaches "basic knowledge and understanding of the regions and countries in the world."

Fletcher, Ruth. *Teaching Peace: Skills for Living in a Global Society*. San Francisco: Harper & Row, 1986. Includes lessons about conflict management, cooperation, interdependence, distribution of resources, and responsible consumerism.

Fluegelman, Andrew, ed. *The New Games Book*. New York: Doubleday, 1976. A collection of games for groups from two to hundreds, most of them designed to be played outdoors simply for fun and the enjoyment of the activity. A personal favorite: "Hunker Hawser," in which players become more vulnerable as they become more aggressive.

Holy Childhood Association, 1720 Massachusetts Avenue, Dept. GA, Washington, DC 20036. HCA is a Catholic educational and fund-raising organization for children that supports Third World projects for children. Ask for free resource guide *In Search of Survival: HCA and Refugee Awareness*. This booklet suggests ways of infusing global awareness into the elementary school curriculum. HCA also publishes a classroom calendar with pictures of children from Third World countries and notations of international holidays.

Heifer Project, Overlook Farm, 216 Wachusett Street, Rutland, MA 01543. An interfaith organization dedicated to "ending world hunger one farmer at a time." Has special programs for children.

Institute for Peace and Justice, 4144 Lindell Boulevard, Room 122, St. Louis, MO 63108; (314) 533-4445. Founded by Jim and Kathy McGinnis, this organization publishes excellent materials on parents and global education. Send for information about the Parenting for Peace and Justice Network.

International Friendship League, 22 Batterymarch Street, Boston, MA 02109. A good resource for pen pals.

Kamii, Constance, and Rheta DeVries. *Group Games in Early Education: Implications for Piaget's Theory.* Washington: National Association for the Education of Young Children, 1980.

Make a World of Difference: Creative Activities for Global Learning. Baltimore: National Council of Churches, Office on Global Education, 1989.

National Catholic Educational Association, 1077 30th Street, NW, Suite 100, Washington, DC 20007. Publishes two resources for assessing schools and religious education programs as instruments of justice and peace education: *Directions for Justice/Peace Education in the Catholic Elementary School* (1985) and *Dimensions of Justice and Peace in Religious Education* (1989). Useful resource for all schools.

The National Geographic Society, Education Services, Department 90, Washington, DC 20036; (800) 368-1718. Ask about the game "Global Pursuit."

Palmer, Parker. *The Company of Strangers: Christians and the Renewal of America's Public Life.* New York: Continuum, 1986.

———. *To Know As We Are Known.* San Francisco: Harper & Row, 1983.

Rogers, Cosby S. and Janet K. Sawyers. *Play in the Lives of Children.* Washington: National Association for the Education of Young Children, 1988.

Social Science Education Consortium, 855 Broadway, Boulder, CO 80302. Send for catalogue of publications, which include *Global Issues in the Elementary Classroom* (1988) and *Global Issues: Activities and Resources for the High School Teacher* (1987). See also *Oh, Garbage! Decisions about Waste Disposal,* a book of creative role-playing exercises.

Social Studies School Service, 10200 Jefferson Boulevard, Room 6, P.O. Box 802, Culver City, CA 90232-0802. Send for a catalogue full of teaching resources, including *Geography in the Newspaper* and many simulation games.

United Nations Association of the USA (UNA-USA), 485 Fifth Avenue, New York, NY 10017-6104; (212) 697-3232. This membership organization promotes support for the United Nations. Ask about the publication

Helping Boys and Girls Discover the World. Although published in 1978 and slightly outdated, this booklet contains several good ideas about infusing global awareness information into the school curriculum. It also suggests ways to teach about the work of the United Nations.

United Nations Public Information Office, United Nations Plaza, New York, NY 10017. Ask for information about UN publications.

Williams, Karen Lynn. *Galimoto.* New York: Lothrop, Lee & Shepard Books. A story for children, ages five to nine, about a seven-year-old in Malawi, who sets out to make his own "galimoto" (the Chichewa word for car) even though he doesn't have enough materials.

World Affairs Materials, Box 726, Kennett Square, PA 19348. Publishes *Catching Up with a Changing World: A Primer on World Affairs*, a popularly written introduction to global issues, and *Twelve Trailblazers of World Community*, essays on ten men and two women who have made significant contributions to global culture. Both written by Leonard S. Kenworthy.

Youth for Understanding (YFU) International Exchange, 3501 Newark Street, NW, Washington, DC 20016-3167. "A private, nonprofit, educational organization dedicated to international understanding and world peace through exchange programs for high school students."

Simulation Games

"Amigos: A Simulation of a Race through Latin America" (Social Studies School Services).

"Bafa Bafa: A Cross Culture Simulation" is designed to give high school students experience in observing and interacting with a different culture (Social Studies School Service).

"Bullets and Ballots" has students role play competing factions in Guatemala during the three months prior to the 1990 presidential election (Social Studies School Service).

"Caravans: An Adventure Simulation Focusing on World Geography" is designed for grades four to eight (Social Studies School Service).

"Civilization Game" introduces students to the techniques used by archaeologists (Social Studies School Service).

"The Debt Game" links hunger, political stability and economics at home and abroad (American Friends Service Committee).

"Gateway: A Simulation of Immigration Issues in Past and Present America" (Social Studies School Service).

"Global Futures Game" has students play the roles of decision makers in world regions (Social Studies School Service).

"Guns or Butter" helps students understand the problems of distribution of limited national resources (Social Studies School Service).

"Hunger on Spaceship Earth" is "the original meal-time simulation game which inspired the so-called hunger dinners that are popular in many churches and schools" (American Friends Service Committee).

"Living in a Global Age" explores issues of global trade and inter-dependence (Social Studies School Service).

"The Maldistribution Simulation" is for senior high school students and adults. It is designed "to have participants experience the realities of the maldistribution of the world's resources and the consequences of such realities" (written by Jim McGinnis, available from Catholic Relief Services).

"Nuclear Escape" has students pose as superpower arms negotiators (Social Studies School Services).

"Rafa Rafa" is a less complex version of "Bafa Bafa" designed for grades four to eight (Social Studies School Service).

"Refugee Camp Life" (*Make a World of Difference*, p. 70).

"Refugee Camp Simulation" (Holy Childhood Association).

"Sharing Food in a Hungry World" (*Make a World of Difference*, p. 100).

"Slave Auction," a simulation set in the southern U.S., in which students role play the slaves, buyers, abolitionists, and auctioneers (Social Studies School Service).

Teaching about Global Awareness with Simulations and Games (Center for Teaching International Relations).

"Who Will Save Abacaxi? A Third World Government Simulation" is a computer simulation for an Apple computer (Social Studies School Service).

"Wildfire II: A Learning Game on the Spread of Nuclear Weapons" (Social Studies School Service).

"World: A Simulation of How Nations Develop and Become Involved in Power Struggles" can be used in grades six through twelve (Social Studies School Service).

Chapter Seven: Teaching Awareness: The Environment

The Body Shop, 45 Horsehill Road, Cedar Knolls, NJ 07927-2003; (800) 541-2535. Offers natural products for skin and hair care. Uses biodegradable ingredients and minimal packaging; rejects animal testing and aerosol sprays; and supports a "Trade not Aid" policy of purchasing ingredients and accessories from the Third World. Catalogue is instructive!

The Children's Rainforest, P.O. Box 936, Lewiston, ME 04240. A nonprofit organization through which children contribute funds to save the Monteverde Cloud Forest in Costa Rica.

Citizen's Clearinghouse for Hazardous Wastes (CCHW), P.O. Box 926, Arlington, VA 22216; (703) 276-7070. Contact CCHW for information about their McToxics campaign, an effort to halt the use of styrofoam in fast food packaging.

Community Products, Inc., Montpelier, VT; (802) 229-1840. Makes "Rain Forest Crunch," a candy like peanut brittle, from pinenuts, Brazil nuts, and cashews from Brazilian rain forests. Offers Brazilian farmers an incentive to harvest rain forest products, not destroy them. Satisfy your sweet tooth while helping the environment! The company is owned by Ben Cohen of Ben and Jerry's ice cream, which has "Rain Forest Crunch" ice cream.

Council on Economic Priorities, 30 Irving Place, New York, NY 10003; (212) 420-1133 or (800) U-CAN-HELP. Publishes *Shopping for a Better World*, a guide that rates the social and environmental performance of over 150 companies. Includes company addresses and names of CEOs.

E: The Environmental Magazine, published bimonthly by Earth Action Network, Inc., P.O. Box 5098, Westport, CT 06881; (203) 854-5559. Subscriptions: P.O. Box 6667, Syracuse, NY 13217. An informative and up-to-date survey of environmentalist issues for the newly-conscious environmentalist as well as the veteran. The ads for ecologically responsible products and services are a welcome change from the alcohol, cigarette, perfume, and automobile ads in most popular magazines.

Earth Island Journal, 300 Broadway, Suite 28, San Francisco, CA 94133; (415) 788-3666. Ask about "Green Pages," a campaign to encourage magazine publishers to plant a tree each time an issue is printed.

Earthworks Group, Box 25, 1400 Shattuck Avenue, Berkeley, CA 94709. Publishes *50 Simple Things You Can Do to Save the Earth*, a good place to start if you're not sure how to begin changing your lifestyle. Sample suggestion: stop junk mail and save trees by getting your name removed from mailing lists. Write to the Mail Preference Service, Direct Marketing Association, 6 East 43rd Street, New York, NY 10017.

Environmental Defense Fund, 257 Park Avenue South, New York, NY 10010; (800) CALL-EDF. Publishes a comprehensive brochure on recycling.

Global ReLeaf, a project of the American Forestry Association, is a global effort that aims to combat the greenhouse effect by using volunteers to plant trees. Write to P.O. Box 2000, Washington, DC 20013 for more information or call (202) 667-3300. Many cities also have tree-planting programs, like TreePeople in Los Angeles, Philadelphia Green, Trees for Houston, and Trees Atlanta. In Africa, several countries celebrate national tree-planting days. In Tanzania, every primary school is required to plant one thousand trees per year for five years. (See "Regreening Tanzania," by Frank Breen, M.M., in *Maryknoll*, vol. 84, no. 1 [January 1990], pp. 12–14.)

Green Committees of Correspondence, P.O. Box 30208, Kansas City, MO 64112; (816) 931-9366. A national clearinghouse for activist environmental groups.

Myers, Norman, ed., *GAIA: An Atlas of Planet Management*. New York: Doubleday, 1984. Illustrated explanations of environmental issues. Shows the interdependence of living things.

Personal Action Guide for the Earth, published by the Transmissions Project for the United Nations Environment Programme (UNEP), 730 Arizona Avenue, #329, Santa Monica, CA 90401. A useful booklet that lists suggestions for personal actions that can contribute to the reduction of environmental problems.

Renewing the Earth, a development education program for adults published by CAFOD, the Catholic Fund for Overseas Development, 2 Romero Close, Stockwell Road, London SW9 9TY. Also published in an edition for youth groups. Available from CRS, c/o Postal Church Service, 8401 Southern Boulevard, Youngstown, OH 44512-6798; (216) 758-4545.

Seventh Generation: Products for a Healthy Planet, 10 Farrell Street, S. Burlington, VT 05403; (800) 456-1177. A small company that markets environmentally responsible products of all kinds. The catalogue is an education in itself!

United Nations Environment Programme (UNEP), North America Office, Room DC2-803, United Nations, NY 10017; (212) 963-8093. Ask for UNEP North America News, a free bimonthly newsletter.

United Nations Association of the United States of America (UNA-USA), 485 Fifth Avenue, New York, NY 10017; (212) 697-3232. This membership organization promotes "constructive U.S. policies on matters of global concern." Ask for information about publications.

Worldwatch Institute, 1776 Massachusetts Avenue, NW, Washington, DC 20036. Publishes a bimonthly magazine, *World Watch*; Worldwatch Papers on selected issues; and an annual report entitled *State of the World*. Goal of its publications is "to help reverse the environmental trends that are undermining the human prospect."

Computer Networks

EcoNet, 3228 Sacramento St., San Francisco, CA 94114; (415) 923-0900. An international environmental telecommunications network.

EnvironNet, free computer network sponsored by Greenpeace Action, Building E, Fort Mason, CA 94123; (415) 474-6767.

Kids Network, a telecommunications-based science and geography curriculum. Contact the National Geographic Society, Educational Services, Department 1001, Washington, DC 20077; (800) 368-2728.

Chapter Eight: Teaching Awareness: Development, Debt, Discrimination

Books

Barton, Carol, and Barbara Weaver. *The Global Debt Crisis: A Question of Justice*. Washington: Interfaith Foundation, 1986. A workbook designed to be used with *From Debt to Development*.

The Debt Crisis Network. *From Debt to Development: Alternatives to the International Debt Crisis*. Washington: Institute for Policy Studies, 1985.

Hollon, Larry. *Selling Human Misery*. Baltimore: National Council of Churches, 1983. A booklet that discusses the "pornography of relief," the exploitation of misery to raise money.

The Hunger Project. *Ending Hunger: An Idea Whose Time Has Come*. New York: Praeger Publishers, 1985. A sourcebook of facts, data, and information about world hunger. Text is comprehensive and photos illustrate the vitality of the people of the Third World.

Mings, Turley. *The Study of Economics: Principles, Concepts and Applications*. Guilford, CT: Dushkin Publishing Group, 1987.

Morgan, Elizabeth. *Global Poverty and Personal Responsibility: Integrity through Commitment*. Mahwah, NJ: Paulist Press, 1989. An excellent introduction to development issues in the Third World.

Renewing the Earth. London: Catholic Fund for Overseas Development, 1989. A study guide that contains a number of development success stories as well as brief explanations of development issues.

The State of the World's Children. Published annually by Oxford University Press for the United Nations Children's Fund (UNICEF), 3 UN Plaza, New York, NY 10017.

Organizations That Can Supply Development Information

Bread for the World, 802 Rhode Island Avenue, NE, Washington, DC 20018.

Catholic Relief Services, Global Education Office, 209 West Fayette Street, Baltimore, MD 21201; (301) 625-2220. Ask for information about the Development Kit.

Center of Concern, 3700 13th Street, NE, Washington, DC 20017.

CODEL, 475 Riverside Drive, Room 1842, New York, NY 10115; (212) 870-3000.

Institute for Food and Development Policy (IFAD), 145 Ninth Street, San Francisco, CA 94103; (415) 864-8555.

Institute for Policy Studies, 1901 Q Street, NW, Washington, DC 20009.

INSTRAW (United Nations International Research and Training Institute for the Advancement of Women), P.O. Box 21747, Santo Domingo, Dominican Republic; (809) 685-2111.

Interfaith Foundation, 110 Maryland Avenue, NE, Suite 509, Washington, DC 20002.

National Council of Churches, Office on Global Education, 2115 North Charles Street, Baltimore, MD 21218-5755.

Overseas Development Council, 1717 Massachusetts Avenue, NW, Washington, DC 20036.

The Stanley Foundation, 216 Sycamore Street, Suite 500, Muscatine, IA 52761.

World Bank Publications, Dept. 0552, Washington, DC 20073-0552. Ask for *Publications Update,* a free, periodic bulletin of publications by the World Bank.

"Socially Conscious" Investment Firms

Calvert Group, 4550 Montgomery Avenue, Suite 1000N, Bethesda, MD 20814; (800) 368-2748.

Pax World Fund, 224 State Street, Portsmouth, NH 03801; (603) 431-8022.

Working Assets Money Fund, 230 California Street, San Francisco, CA 94111; (415) 989-3200.

Also contact the Funding Exchange, 135 East 15th Street, New York, NY 10003 for a copy of its "Directory of Socially Responsible Investment."

Index

~

141